The Arab Radicals

The Arab Radicals

Adeed Dawisha

COUNCIL ON FOREIGN RELATIONS BOOKS

Copyright © 1986 by the Council on Foreign Relations, Inc.
All rights reserved.
Printed in the United States of America.

Library of Congress Cataloging-in-Publication Data

Dawisha, A. I.
    The Arab radicals.

    Includes index.
    1. Arab countries—Politics and government—1945–
I. Title.
DS63.1.D39   1986   909'.09749270828   86-19733
ISBN 0-87609-020-X
ISBN 0-87609-019-6 (pbk.)

For Nadia and Emile,
who helped keep the book short

Contents

Foreword

Those who have dealt with the Middle East over the years often use "moderate" and "radical" to characterize regimes and organizations in the region. While those terms serve as quick, shorthand points of reference, they also can be misleading about the origins, motivations, and present aims of participants, movements, and national states in the area. Because these words will continue to be used by journalists, speechwriters, and policymakers, it is important to reflect on what they do and do not mean.

This book places the word "radical" into historical and current Middle Eastern contexts. It helps us understand the roots, aims, and diversity of states and movements called "radical." After reading the book, few reflective readers will feel comfortable in using words like "radical" and "terrorist" indiscriminately to put large groups outside the circle of those with whom thoughtful policymakers must deal.

Professor Dawisha quite properly starts with a broad definition of "radical" designed to approximate the meaning intended in the common use of the word. This has one advantage and one disadvantage which all of us face in using such words.

He describes "radicalism" as an attitude of mind leading to a course of action bent on undermining and changing the established political order. That is a reasonable definition which both encompasses groups within a state—even a radical state—determined to change the system within that state, and states bent on reaching across borders with some sort of revolutionary purpose to change the system in other states.

He does not attempt to define the *degree* and *kind* of change by which some might differentiate between "fundamental reform" and "radicalism." He correctly observes that we Americans have a tendency to associate "'radicalism' . . . with the concept of political and social change, and more often than not with rapid change" and, for many of us, "within this context, the term 'radical' characterizes the ideas and actions of groups that work to overthrow an established political order; of countries and regimes that aim to un-

dermine the political authority and legitimacy of other states and regimes; and of states seeking to modify or change existing power relationships in an international system," preferably by force.

Social and political change—even rapid change—is part of life
in today's world. The Middle East in the 1970s—particularly in the
oil-producing states—was one of the most rapidly changing areas
of the developing world; existing social patterns continuing to un-
dergo substantial transformation. Yet we do not call these changes
"radical" because "radicalism" also involves an element of tearing
up a system by its roots—often through violent and sudden action—and replacing it with a system having new characteristics.

The distinction is important to keep in mind as we read Professor Dawisha's book. It is also essential to keep in mind that "radical" states and movements may quickly change their character or
appearance as events evolve and the environment changes. He observes that a state like Iraq, which may correctly be discussed in a
chapter on "radical" states because of historical actions and the
stated philosophy of its ruling party, may turn to pragmatic policies
which justify a pragmatic response by other governments. Members of an organization like the Palestine Liberation Organization
may find their early intellectual roots in philosophies of armed
struggle which at one time offered a way of changing an unjust situation. But, if these Palestinians were to state their readiness to
change that situation by negotiating peace with Israel and turning
their energies to building their own permanent political institutions, would they still be radical?

It is also true that "radicalism" is often in the eye of the behol-
der and is often used with positive connotations only by certain parties. Despite the intent of the Afghan resistance to overthrow the
present Communist regime in Kabul, or of the aim of Jonas
Savimbi's UNITA to overthrow the existing government in Angola,
or of the Contras' or Solidarity's objectives of changing the character and focus of governments in Nicaragua or Poland, few
policymakers in Washington would describe those groups as "radical."

Professor Dawisha's book challenges the policymaker to shar-
pen his or her performance in several important areas:

First, his analysis makes clear that the U.S. policymakers cannot afford to write off a particular government or organization be-

cause it is called "radical" or to count on one because it is labeled "moderate." These labels are often the tools of the lobbyist and the political assassin. They are inappropriate bases for policy. It is a primary contribution of Professor Dawisha's work to cause those who analyze, make, or vote on American policy to think carefully about what they mean when they call a state, movement, or organization "radical."

The task of the policymaker is to probe exactly what aims a government is pursuing at a particular time and then construct a pragmatic test to determine the extent to which we can work together if there is reason to try. Syria provides a good example—signatory of the May 1974 disengagement with Israel mediated by the U.S., scrupulous adherent to understanding on preventing terrorist acts across that border, adversary in Lebanon, possible supporter of terrorist acts, divider of the PLO, protector of Syria's interests in its neighborhood, in and out of friendly relations with Jordan. The challenge to the policymaker is to probe actively to determine how to test whether, when, and where we share common interest.

Second, policymakers must begin with an understanding that change is inevitable, and focus more precisely on how change is accomplished. An important criterion for judging the compatibility of a regime may well be how it manages change, including its respect for the rights of its citizens.

It is only by focusing early on the pressures for political and social changes that we will begin thinking about how governments can deal with those pressures in constructive rather than destructive ways. The question Professor Dawisha's analysis poses is whether a government approaches change in a radical way because of its inherent character or because it lacks constructive alternatives. No one should expect that the United States can define the terms of change around the world, but if the United States is not to be seen only as a "status quo power" but as a country which supports constructive reform and change, we will have to be more explicit about our philosophy of change and its aims.

Third, we will have to be more astute in our political analysis of societies where pressure for change is mounting. This, again, is not to say that the United States has the capacity to prescribe or influence political change in countries around the world. But U.S. policymakers must be in a position to distinguish between political elements pressing to conserve what is best in a system and to reform it and elements bent on tearing up the system and replacing it with one which would eventually restrict the freedom of its people and its future ability to change and adjust to the domestic and international circumstances. Judgments of this kind come down in the end to an accurate understanding of who is engineering change and how political power is being exercised as it changes hands. Judgments may also depend on mechanisms that will permit peaceful evolutionary change to continue as important constituencies make ongoing judgments on the responsiveness of their changing political system.

Does the United States—a nation whose philosophy was once called "revolutionary" for good reason and whose people live in one of the fastest changing societies of the world today—always want to be listed as a "status quo" power? We do a reasonably good job of managing change at home, but when we face change abroad the immediate instinct of many policymakers is to regard it as the handiwork of "radicals" and to think only of how to stop it. There are, indeed, "radicals" whose approach to change may be destructive. There are also those who may seek urgent change who are still willing to seek peaceful, just, and constructive ways to accomplish change. Professor Dawisha's study challenges policymakers to understand the difference before they act.

Harold H. Saunders

Preface

On October 23, 1983, a suicide truck loaded with an estimated 5,000 pounds of explosives crashed through the
headquarters of the United States marine batallion in
Beirut. When the carnage had finally been cleared, America was
stunned to learn that 241 of its marines had lost their lives. Indeed,
the writing had been on the wall for some time. Six months earlier,
on April 18, a bomb had exploded at the United States embassy in
Beirut, killing 63 people and injuring almost 100, and completely
destroying the central consular section of the building. Seventeen
of those killed were American nationals, including marine guards,
senior embassy staff, and the director of the C.I.A.'s office for the
Near East and South Asia, along with six other C.I.A. personnel.
These two acts were perhaps the primary catalyst for America's
eventual withdrawal from Lebanon. They were attributed to radical
Islamic Shiites.

Similarly, it was the radical Shiite zealots of Southern Lebanon,
rather than the Arab states' armed forces, who inflicted on Israel its
first major defeat in the area. Having totally failed to impose its will
on the South of Lebanon, and with its army's morale at its lowest
ebb because of the unremitting hostility of the Lebanese Shiites, the
Israeli cabinet voted in January 1985 to withdraw unilaterally and
unconditionally from Lebanon.

In the wake of these events, American attitudes toward Middle
East politics seemed to shift quickly and perceptibly. In the 1970s,
Washington's problem-solving emphasis was focused on state-to-
state relations. Much effort was placed on trying to effect a political
settlement between Israel and the Arab *states*; and when this
seemed difficult to achieve, the United States ensured that Israel's
military dominance over the Arab *states* was maintained.

Increasingly in the 1980s, however, America became preoc-
cupied, even obsessed, with the hostile acts perpetrated against it
by radical groups, sometimes supported and abetted by certain
states in the area. And in American eyes, these groups seemed determined to attack American citizens, institutions and interests not

only within, but also beyond, the confines of the Middle East region. Frustrated by its inability to fight the shadowy forces of "terrorism," Washington adopted a policy of military retaliation against
states sponsoring terrorist groups—hence the attack on Libya in
April 1986.

This book grew out of a Council on Foreign Relations study of
the forces of radicalism in the Arab world. The choice of the topic
was naturally influenced by the seemingly unending and virulent
hostility of the radical forces toward not only Israel and the United
States, but also the moderate, status-quo Arab states in the 1970s
and 1980s. But from the outset, the book was never intended to address itself to the narrow issue of terrorism, which is no more than
an instrument of policy. The book has a much broader scope: it is an
analysis of the institutions, motives and activities of the radical
Arab states and movements, some, perhaps most, of whom have
used terrorism as an instrument of their radical policies.

The book, furthermore, starts from the premise that the main
target of the Arab radicals in the 1970s and 1980s has not been the
United States. The goals of the radicals have been more limited, directed primarily at the immediate political environment, the Middle
East. And if the United States has become a frequent target, it is because it is perceived as a consistent supporter of the opponents of
Arab radicalism, namely the status-quo Arab states and Israel.

I am indebted to a number of people who helped at various
stages in this endeavour. In the early part of the study, a number of
prominent scholars presented papers on various aspects of "Arab
radicalism" to a study group that convened at the Council on
Foreign Relations from December 1984 to April 1985. I benefited
greatly from these presentations and the ensuing discussions. But
the book is neither a summation, nor a representation, of the
group's views. I alone am responsible for the analysis that follows,
which is based primarily on my own independent research, and re-
flects my long-held assumptions about the bases and conduct of
Arab radical politics. Lisa Anderson, John Campbell, Peter Grose,
Paul Jabber, David Lawrence, Bernard Lewis, Dennis Mullin and
James Piscatori participated in an author's review committee, ably
chaired by Paul Kreisberg. Their comments on an earlier draft went
a long way toward improving the final version. Special thanks are
also due to Charles Issawi and J. C. Hurewitz who chaired the study

group meetings and to Eleanor Tejirian who acted as the group's rapporteur. John Kagian and Christina Condon, my research assistants during my tenure at the Woodrow Wilson International Center for Scholars in 1985–86, took major responsibility for preparing the appendix—an arduous and thankless undertaking for which I am very thankful. I am grateful too to David Kellogg, the Publications Director, and Robert Valkenier and Patricia Dockham, the editors, for their skill, expertise and resourcefulness. And last but not least, my thanks go to Mary Ann Barone, Joyce Donahue, Susanne Roach, Alice McCloughlin and Terry Calway, who typed various drafts of the manuscript with great speed and efficiency.

Members of the Council on Foreign Relations' study group on "Arab Radicalism" were: Mr. Morris B. Abram, Professor Fouad Ajami, Hon. James E. Akins, Professor Lisa Anderson, Professor Carl Brown, Dr. Norman Cigar, Mr. Arnaud de Borchgrave, Mr. Donald T. Fox, Mr. Melvin A. Goodman, Mr. Joseph N. Greene, Jr., Mr. Richard C. Hottelet, Dr. J.C. Hurewitz, Dr. Charles Issawi, Dr. Paul Jabber, Ms. Tamar Jacoby, Dr. Rashid Khalidi, Dr. Zalmay Khalilzad, Dr. Nicola N. Khuri, Lt. Gen. Richard Lawrence, Professor Bernard Lewis, Mr. John H. Lichtblau, Hon. Richard H. Nolte, Dr. Daniel Pipes, Maj. Patrick A. Putignano, Dr. William B. Quandt, Mr. Arnold Raphel, Professor Nadav Safran, Dr. Gary G. Sick, Mr. Jack B. Sunderland, Mr. Howard R. Teicher, Ms. Eleanor Tejirian, Professor A. L. Udovich, Mr. Robert J. White, Hon. W. Howard Wriggins, and Professor I. William Zartman.

Particular thanks are due the authors of the discussion papers prepared for the Council's study group: Lisa Anderson ("Arab Radicalism: The Libyan Case"); Kamal Beyoghlow ("Arab Radicalism: The Case of the Syrian Arab Republic"); Norman Cigar ("Arab Radicalism: The Case of South Yemen"); John P. Entelis ("Algeria in World Politics"); Rashid Khalidi ("The PLO . . . and Palestinian Radicalism"); and Augustus Richard Norton ("The Amal Movement in Lebanon").

Adeed Dawisha

May 1986

The Arab Radicals

Part One

Introduction

1
Arab Radicalism: A Clarification

In a commercial on American television, a comfortable-looking man of means, sitting in an elegant reading room among other self-assured representatives of middle-class America, tells the viewer that a particular corporation has begun to try out "something rather radical." At this point, his confident and content colleagues in the room abruptly turn to the camera with their mouths wide open, with horror blanketing their eyes. Only when the "something rather radical" turns out to be a device designed to improve the efficiency of the free market economy, do eyes smile and faces relax.

Few people are better than the advertisers of Madison Avenue at gauging and reflecting the public mood. And there is little doubt that America of the 1980s is a society that increasingly perceives the notion of radicalism as antithetical to cherished American values. Thus when American leaders and opinion-makers persist in reducing complex global relationships into the comfortingly simple formulation of "friends vs. foes," America's friends are usually (admittedly not always) seen and depicted as "moderate" and "peace loving," and when they are not, they are at least "benign"; whereas the country's foes are projected as "violent" (lately, "terroristic"), "evil" and decidedly "radical."

It is not that such characterizations are necessarily erroneous. A quick scan of the "international radical scene" does indeed suggest that, on balance, the radicals overwhelmingly seem to be at odds with American global interest. And the Arab world is no exception to this rule. Whether manifested by a popular song in the 1950s inviting Secretary of State John Foster Dulles to dance rock 'n' roll on his Sixth Fleet rather than on Arab soil, or by fiery religious sermons in the 1980s reminding President Reagan that his "satanic" policies are fated to rebound on his own country and his own people, Arab radicalism frequently, almost consistently, has found itself in a state of confrontation with American interests and goals in the area.

But the main target of post-World War II Arab radicalism, whether of the nationalist or religious variety, has not been the United States. The goals of the high priests of Arab radicalism have always been much more limited, much more local, directed primarily at the immediate political environment. It is the Middle East, and particularly the Arab world, which has constituted the main arena where the struggles and compromises, the triumphs and defeats, of Arab radicalism have been played out since the mid-1950s.

It is true that with the gradual eclipse of the two colonial powers, Britain and France, in the 1950s, the United States became the standard bearer of Western interests in the area, thus devolving upon itself a role that was bound to be antithetical to the premises and promises of Arab radicalism. From the mid-1950s onward, it was America that became the object of the Arabs' historically based and deeply felt mistrust and fear of the West. Yet, history only tended to reinforce the suspicions created primarily by American policies judged to be hostile to the goals and aspirations of the Arab radicals. It has been the consistent American support for the opponents of Arab radicalism—namely the status quo Arab countries and Israel—that has been Washington's primary sin in the eyes of Arab radicals.

well, naturally

Arab radicalism's primary concern is with the Arab world and the Middle East. And it is this theater of operations with which I shall be primarily concerned in this book. Concentrating mainly, but not entirely, on the 1970s and 1980s, I shall endeavor to identify the Arab radicals and their institutions, delve into their motives and ideologies, and analyze their policies and activities. Implicit are a

number of recurring questions that I try to deal with in the various
parts of the book—questions such as: What is there in the recent
history of the radical states and organizations in the Arab world that
nurtured radicalism? What are the institutions that underpin, legitimate, support and implement radical policies? What role does the
perennial Arab phenomenon of personalized authoritarian politics
play in the maintenance and encouragement of radicalism? Are
leaders of radical forces genuinely radical, or do they use radicalism
to legitimate their role? What is the impact on Arab radicalism of external actors, particularly Israel, Iran, the United States and the
Soviet Union? What are the prospects that radicalism will expand or
diminish within the state-dominated Arab political order? And
what factors can we identify in order to map the future course and
direction of radicalism in the Arab world?

But what constitutes radicalism? For the purpose of this book, I
shall define "radicalism" as an attitude of mind encompassing a
course of action that aims, for whatever reasons, to undermine and
possibly transform the status quo. The term, therefore, is intrinsically associated with the concept of political and social change, and
more often than not with rapid change. It also involves an element
of tearing up a system by its roots—often through violent action—
and replacing it with a system having new characteristics. Within
this context, the term "radical" characterizes the ideas and actions
of groups that work to overthrow an established political order; of
countries and regimes that aim to undermine the political authority
and legitimacy of other states and regimes; and of states seeking to
modify or change existing power relationships in an international
system.

Such a definition is meant to be not only value-free, but also devoid of simplistic emotive characterizations. Neither positive nor
negative values are placed on the notions of status quo and change.
Thus, the Marxist-Leninist concept of the "dictatorship of the pro-
letariat" was indeed a radical assault on the order of things as they
existed in the nineteenth and early twentieth centuries. But then,
by our definition, so was John Locke's seventeenth century impas-
sioned plea for individual liberty and for the sovereignty of the
people a radical attack on both the intellectual status quo as represented then by the absolutist ideas of Thomas Hobbes and the
political status quo of the autocratic rule of James II, backed by a

Church of England preaching the divine rights of sovereigns.[1] Similarly, any revolution aiming to transform the political and socio-economic system (and not just to remove from power those who distort the system—e.g., Ferdinand Marcos in the Philippines)—whether its underlying ideology is republican-egalitarian (the French Revolution), Marxist-Leninist (the Russian and Chinese Revolutions), Fascist-Nazi (the Italian and German revolutions), or Islamic (the Iranian Revolution)—is considered, within my terms of reference, a radical event.

What constitutes the political status quo in the Arab world today? At the state level, the status quo is represented by the regime or the government of the day. It is immaterial how a particular regime came to power, or indeed how popular or democratic it happens to be, so long as it has the power to interpret the national interest and to formulate and enact policies based on this interpretation. As long as it is able to provide basic services and maintain public order, then, Machiavellian as this may seem, the regime will be considered as constituting the status quo. And individuals and groups trying to overthrow the regime and undermine the political order of their particular state are termed radical.

Beyond the domain of the state, there is the interstate level of the Arab regional system as a whole, as it operates within the larger context of Middle East politics. In this system the status quo is a conglomerate of sovereign states represented by their national governments (and also the Palestine Liberation Organization which, for all intents and purposes, is accorded the status and legitimacy of a government-in-exile), the majority of which conduct their relations in accordance with accepted sets of rules and norms of behavior that are generally enshrined in the U.N. Charter as well as in the Charter of the League of Arab States. Articles 5, 6 and 8 of the Arab League Charter (which became its most important sections) prohibit not only aggression and the use of force by member-states against each other, but also interference by one Arab state in the internal affairs of another.[2] Any state or group that has worked to undermine, or at least adhered to an ideology prescribing the subversion of, the established regional Arab order is termed radical.

Now while these are the primary inter-Arab criteria by which Arab radicals are distinguished from the non-radicals, they are not the only ones, for there are other features that lie outside the Arab world that ought to characterize the policies and behavior of the Arab radicals. "Militancy" and "steadfastness"* vis-à-vis the question of Israel and Palestinian rights is one such condition. The nonradicals, of course, seek change in the regional status quo vis-à-vis Israel, but they differ from the radicals in an essential way. The very nature of the radical creed assumes that those forces that intermittently or frequently challenge the Arab status quo system domestically or on a regional basis cannot but rule out any compromises with Israel as it is constituted territorially and ideologically at present. Thus the absolute minimum that these radicals would demand is that no agreement with the Jewish state should be reached until a true military/strategic parity (preferably superiority) is achieved, and until Israel makes a clear declaration that it intends to withdraw completely from all the territories it occupied in the June 1967 Arab-Israeli war. The maximum demand, of course, would be the complete dismantling of the Jewish state and in its place the creation of a Palestinian-Arab state. Each radical group or country would naturally have its own agenda for the composition and ideological orientation of the future Palestinian state.

Because of the close ideological and strategic association between the United States on the one side and Israel and the regional status quo order in the Arab world on the other, "anti-Americanism" seems to have become a characteristic that more often than not is associated with a true radical orientation.[3] America is seen not only as the protector, and ultimately the guarantor, of Israel's "expansionism," which is bad enough in itself, but also as the real source of many of the failures and the "capitulationist" attitudes and policies of the Arab status quo powers. It is, for example, instructive that even a group such as the Muslim Brotherhood, which has waged an intermittently violent struggle against the pro-Soviet regime of Hafiz al-Assad in Syria for over ten years, has shied away from, indeed worked vigorously to dispel suspicion of, any identification with the Soviet Union's major political and ideological foe, the United States.

---

*From the Arabic al-sumood, meaning to stand up to pressure—in this case, the perceived pressure of Israeli and American interests and ambitions in the area.

Where does the Soviet Union itself fit into all this? There is little doubt that partly because of the Arab radicals' anti-Americanism, partly because of an overlap in outlooks and political orientations, and partly because of a congruence of political interests, many Arab radicals have tended to be allied to, or at least be supported by, the Soviet Union. By no means, however, has this been a universal phenomenon. Indeed, even at the height of Soviet "penetration" of the Arab world in the period 1955–73, there was always dormant tension between the Arab radicals, committed as they were to the ideals of Arab nationalism, and the internationalist creed of Soviet Marxism-Leninism. With the increasing prominence of radical Islamic states and groups in the Middle East in the 1970s, the Soviet Union's adherence to a publicly promoted atheistic ideology has tended to undermine its ability to penetrate the hearts and minds of the Islamic radicals. Because of Arabism and Islam, therefore, Soviet influence on the Arab radicals has been, and will continue to be, a transient affair, selectively located and temporarily felt, built not on cultural or ideological proximity, but on political expedience operative at a particular period of time.[4] Indeed, the hostility of the Islamic radicals is as great (sometimes even greater) to the Soviet Union as it is to the United States.[5] Because of all this, and contrary to views sometimes expressed in the West, I do not regard the "Soviet connection" as a necessary element for defining Arab radicalism.

With these criteria in mind, we can conclude that the main Arab radical forces comprise the states of Libya, Syria, South Yemen, Algeria and Iraq, and the organizations of the Palestine Liberation Organization, the Shiite Amal movement and its derivatives Hizbollah and Islamic Jihad in Lebanon as well as the Da'wa party in Iraq, and the primary Sunni Muslim Brotherhood organizations and their smaller, more militant offshoots operating in Egypt and in Syria. These states and groups constitute what in this book will be referred to as the Arab radicals.

I do not mean to suggest that these groups are the only radical actors in the Arab and Middle Eastern political theatre. Certain lesser groups that follow radical policies and engage in terrorism lie beyond the purview of this study. Some are peripheral to the Arab world at large—e.g. the Druze in Lebanon. Others, to which intermittent references will be made, are shadowy cell-like factions that are difficult to analyze because so little is known about them. Nor am I concerned with every single manifestation of dissent in Arab countries. Demonstrations, strikes, occasional clashes with security forces by students, workers, members of outlawed and largely insignificant organizations—e.g. the Communist Party, obviously are radical acts. However, my concern is not to write an encyclopedia of Middle Eastern radical activity, but to concentrate on the groups (and their actions) that, since 1970, have constituted at various times *real* and *significant* threat to domestic and/or regional status quo.

It is important to emphasize, however, that by labeling the above countries and organizations radical, I do not imply that all have been equally radical, or that each has been consistently radical from 1970 to the present. On the contrary, Arab radicalism can be conceived of as a continuum over time and space. At one extremity lie the most consistently radical actors (for example, Libya and the Syrian Muslim Brothers). At the other end, I place those states and organizations which have been radical at one time but have become moderate (or vice versa), or which have taken radical positions on some issues but shown moderation on others (for example, Iraq, Algeria, and even in some ways, the PLO).

In illustration, let me cite the case of Iraq. Under the definitional criteria, it can be argued that up until 1977 Iraq was one of the most consistently radical states in the Arab world, but that from 1978 onward the Iraqi leaders moderated their position so that by 1984 Iraq had become almost a status quo power. How then do I justify the inclusion of Iraq in the radical camp? Two primary reasons can be given. In the first place, as has been indicated, when the entire period from 1970 till the present is analyzed, not an insubstantial part of that period was characterized by radical Iraqi policies and activities in the region. Second, while Iraq has moderated its policies in some areas, particularly over the issue of noninterference in the internal affairs of other Arab countries, it remains publicly committed, at least in principle, to the revolutionary ideology of the Baath Party as enunciated in the party's charter and the resolutions of the various party congresses. Until there is a conscious and public rejection of Baathism, or at least a redefinition of its revolutionary dimensions, there can be no guarantee that the moderation of the 1980s is permanent and not simply a transient phase dic-

tated by certain political expediencies. For these reasons, I have
called Iraq a radical Arab country.

On the broader issue, is it credible to postulate a concept of
Arab radicalism that can penetrate state borders and put aside, at
least occasionally, differences between Sunni and Shia, and Muslim and Christian? The term "Arab radicalism" assumes that there
exists a sense of Arabness, which makes it difficult to discuss its
manifestation in only one country or movement without reference
to the rest of the Arab world. And indeed there is linkage throughout the region because of the continuing symbolic potency, despite
the recent Islamic challenge, of the concept of Arabism among the
peoples of the various contemporary Arab states.

Arabism need not necessarily mean a movement toward political unity, as prescribed in pan-Arabist writings before the 1967
Arab-Israeli War. Here, the term refers to an awareness of Arab
identity, "of belonging to a vast group supposed to share a common
origin, characterized by a name and by common cultural features,
and above all by all the bounds of the linguistic community."[6]
Arabism, as such, may not be powerful enough to overcome the
many schisms and differences that exist among the peoples and
leaders of the Arab world and, therefore, cannot on its own drive
them toward the road of organic unity. Yet, as an idea and a symbol
it is potent enough to set cultural, even normative, standards with
which most citizens of Arab countries tend to identify. In the most
sophisticated public opinion survey in the Arab world to date, a
group of Arab social scientists set out to investigate the potency of
Arabism among the people of the Arab countries. The findings,
published in 1980,[7] showed that eight out of ten respondents believed that the Arabs belonged to a single nation, and that they
were culturally distinctive. Moreover, six out of ten favored greater
Arab cooperation, which they saw as ultimately moving the various
Arab countries and groups to a future federal union.[8] In this kind of
cultural milieu, radicalism, even when it operates strictly within a
country, will have its influence felt beyond the restrictive confines
of state borders.

Finally, what of Islam? Like Arabism, it acts as a universal normative force whose impact and influence cut across the boundaries
of Arab states. Not only is Islam the religion of the overwhelming
majority of the Arab people, but when Arabs look back into the an-

nals of their history, they cannot but be struck by the fact that the richest heritage of their history arose in the years of the vast and vibrant Arab Islamic empire. Consequently, the acknowledgment of the influence of Islam in Arab society is not confined to the traditional and conservative Arab states, but also extends to the revolutionary and radical Arab countries and movements. As such, not only can Islam be interpreted so as to motivate radical action on the popular level throughout the Arab world, but also it can act as the medium through which the radical creed is transmitted across national boundaries.

This, of course, does not mean that within the realm of Islam and Arabism there are no divisions, that people cherish the same values and fight for the same causes. Indeed, one argument posits that the real radicalism in the Arab world of the 1980s is not that professed by states along traditional Arab concerns such as the question of Palestine. Rather, it is a religious/economic struggle between the disinherited and the possessors of wealth and power; between, in some cases, the Sunni political order and the Shiite popular order, and in other cases between the secular ruling elites and the dispossessed masses clinging to religious fundamentalism for their ultimate political and economic salvation. Accordingly, esoteric problems of foreign policy are but a diversion from the central issue of the distribution of wealth and power; and the real radicals are those who are on the fringes of the established order, struggling to inherit power, money and land.

While this argument is by no means false, it is somewhat limited in its scope. Its emphasis is primarily domestic, concentrating on the traditional divide between rulers and ruled, elites and masses. It neither takes into consideration inter-state conflict within the Arab world itself, nor the perennial Arab-Israeli confrontation. Israel and the Palestinian problem is hardly an esoteric foreign policy issue for the Arab people. It is, and has always been, a matter of concern for the majority of Arabs, irrespective of their state, class, or political affiliation. And in any case, limited as it is, this argument does not fall beyond the conceptual parameters of my definition, in the sense that it looks at and emphasizes the seeds of rebellion against the socio-economic and political status quo.

One further point needs to be stressed. The period that I am concerned with here is the contemporary one, spanning the years from 1970 to the present. Of course, contemporary Arab radicalism did not begin in 1970, but has its roots in many decades of intermittent radical agitation and activity. Most immediately relevant to the concern of this study is the post-World War II period, particularly the 1950s, when partly because of their defeat at the hands of the new state of Israel in 1948–49, and partly because of the persistence of the colonial order, the Arabs, especially the urban modernizing elite, began to rebel against the established order. Revolutionary movements and ideologies such as Baathism, Arab Nationalism, Communism and, most potent of all, Nasserism found in the hearts and minds of Arabs of that period fertile ground for penetration and growth.

That phase of Arab radicalism, however, had spent itself by 1970. Although the decline had set in earlier, the demise was considerably accelerated by what can only be described as the seminal event in contemporary Arab history, the June 1967 Arab-Israeli War. The radicals of the 1950s, mainly young modernizing and nationalist military officers who embodied the aspirations of the nationalist generation, miserably failed to deliver on that most central of Arab nationalist concerns, the Palestinian issue. Years of revolutionary rhetoric and promises of final deliverance produced nothing more than yet another ignominious defeat at the hands of the supposedly "illegitimate and inconsequential Zionist entity." People's frustrations and anger were aimed at the radical leaders who had promised much but delivered little. And even those who continued to control the levers of political power in the aftermath of the June 1967 War were no longer able to reside in the hearts of their people.

The culmination of this process of decline came in 1970 with the death of President Gamal Abd al-Nasser of Egypt and the overthrow, by Hafiz al-Assad, of the neo-Marxist Salah Jadid in Syria. In the meantime, much had changed in other parts of the Arab world. The Baath Party took control in Iraq in 1968, and in the same year South Yemen, under the Marxist leadership of its National Liberation Front, gained its independence. Muamar Qadhafi emerged as leader in Libya in 1969 and proceeded, after Nasser's death, to support materially and militarily the extreme Muslim revolutionary movements, which, long active in Egypt, were coming into prominence and acquiring new adherents in other parts of the Arab world during the 1970s. The Palestine Liberation Organization came of age as a feared and powerful actor on the Arab political scene after the battle in March 1968 in which Palestinian commandos inflicted heavy losses on a large Israeli force sent to destroy guerrilla bases in the town of Karameh in East Jordan. The PLO's defeat by the Jordanian army in September 1970, after establishing what was essentially a state within a state, is another reason for positing 1970 as the starting point for this study of the Arab radicals. Expelled from Jordan, the Palestinian guerrillas moved en masse to Lebanon—an event which had far-reaching radical consequences for the region as a whole.

The picture of Arab radicalism, therefore, is a complex one in which a variety of objectives are sought and different strategies are played out in a turbulent period of Arab politics. But ultimately, whichever way and in whatever context radicalism is perceived, its definition as a movement determined to challenge the Arab status quo, whether inside a particular Arab country or within the Arab regional state system, and to undermine Israeli and American interests in the area, remains theoretically and operatively valid. And it is on the bases of this definition that the following analysis should afford us the opportunity to compare and contrast individual cases, and to reach a broad understanding of the general phenomenem of Arab radicalism and its impact on Middle Eastern politics and international relations.

One final conceptual clarification remains. With the present Western obsession about the spread of terrorism, many may wonder how the two concepts of radicalism and terrorism interrelate, and to what extent the book will address itself to the spate of terrorist activities perpetrated mainly by Palestinian and Shiite zealots against Israeli and Western targets, and supported overtly and covertly by Iran and some radical Arab states.

Let me therefore state at the outset that this book is not about terrorism and its psychology per se. Nor is it about the practical means by which terrorist activities can be combatted. Those seeking advice on such measures as enhancing airport security and protecting government buildings will find none here. This book is an analysis of the structure, motives and activities of the radical Arab states and movements, some of which undoubtedly have used terrorism as an instrument of their radical policies. Inherent in the analysis are suggestions not of means to thwart terrorism but rather of ways to encourage change in the motivation that spurs such violence.

It is essential first to distinguish between terrorism and radicalism. Whereas terrorism constitutes one of various instruments of policy, albeit a very potent one, radicalism embodies the very essence of the policy itself, as well as the values, goals and concerns of those who formulate and implement policies. For example, the PLO may officially disclaim terrorism in certain circumstances, preferring instead the diplomatic path. But it cannot disclaim radicalism, for to do so would be to relinquish the Palestinians' aim to overturn the status quo and establish, by any means deemed necessary, a Palestinian state of some kind. And it is the radicalism and those aims, rather than the terrorism per se, of the PLO which the Israelis fear most.

Following from the above, it is important to understand that notwithstanding the sadistic few who perpetrate violence for the sake of violence, terrorism is ultimately used to achieve political and/or ideological ends. In the Middle Eastern cycle of violence, there are perhaps as many villains as there are victims; all of them— be they Muslims, Christians or Jews, be they individuals, groups, or states—come equipped with reasoned, more often than not sophisticated, arguments about the sanctity of their cause and the necessity of their violent methods. And beyond that, there is little doubt that terrorism is also used to settle personal scores among governments and leaders, radical and moderate, pro-Soviet and pro-Western, who operate in a conflict-ridden region.

Terrorism is thus by no means the domain solely of the radical Arabs. Nor is it easy for the serious and balanced analyst to draw a clear moral and philosophical distinction between an attack on an enemy target in a foreign airport that claims the lives of bystanders and a bombing raid on enemy concentrations in a crowded city that also results in the death of non-combatants. Nevertheless, there can be no doubt that many abhorrent acts of terrorism have been committed by radical Arab groups, acts that have been applauded, supported, sometimes facilitated, by such radical states as Syria and Libya.

While not addressing itself to the narrow issue of terrorist activities as an instrument of policy, this book, by analyzing the motives, institutions and activities of Arab radicalism, should offer some clues to those who seek to understand why some states or groups resort to various means of violence, including acts that claim the lives of innocent civilians and political bystanders.

Lybia
Syria
S. yemen
Algria
Iraq
Shiite - Amal
Islamic Jihad,
Hizbollah
PLO

Problem of Arabness — lack of focus on states —

2
The Radical Legacy of Anti-Westernism

I f there is one dominant American image pertaining to the Arab world today, it is that of the Arab radical as an individual who is almost instinctively anti-American. And as I have argued in the first chapter, there certainly are some bases for this image. When Americans endeavor to understand the causes of this Arab hostility to U.S. policies and intentions, their accusing fingers point to an "authoritarian" and "violent" culture, diametrically opposed to cherished American values, and egged on by the hidden (and not so hidden) hand of Soviet expansionism.

Such assessments reduce a much more complex reality into almost meaningless generalizations. They also lack historical perspective, which is unfortunate, since the "only hope of discerning the forces actually operative in the [contemporary] world is to range them firmly against the past."[1] It is indeed in the present that policies are formulated, implemented and make their impact on a people's psyche. But this psyche is no virgin land: it is the repository of national images, symbols, even myths, which in their totality constitute the collective memory of a people. However, the analyst of contemporary life must use history intelligently: not everything in the past is relevant, not everything is constant. The analyst should discern from history those patterns and contours of human behavior that continue in some ways to influence the contemporary world around him. And there can be little doubt that post-World War II Arab radicalism, particularly in its avowedly anti-Western orientation, has its roots in the way Arabs perceive not only the development of their long history, but also their historical relations with the West.

One of the most powerful and enduring factors of contemporary Arab life has been the Arabs' attachment to the memory of their glorious past. The period that spanned the rise of the Arab/Islamic civilization in the seventh century and its eventual eclipse in the fifteenth century is seen by most Arabs as the epitome of Arab and Islamic endeavor, constituting their own substantial offering to the progress of human civilization and proof of what Arabs are capable of.

In the military domain the power of the Muslim Arabs struck fear in people's hearts. Indeed, during the first century after the birth of Islam the Arabs had expanded their realm from Central Asia and Northern India in the east to Spain in the West. Intellectually, while Europe languished in the darkness of the medieval ages, Baghdad of the Abbasids, Cairo of the Fatimids, Qairawan of the North African Aghlabids and Cordoba of the Andalusian Ummayads were the lively cultural centers of a Muslim world that established and maintained a significant influence upon Western scientific and literary thought. For it was essentially Muslim scholars of the vibrant Arab empires who "developed the philosophic and scientific heritage of ancient Asia, Egypt, Persia and India, brought it into line with the religious precepts of a monotheistic world, and so provided the essential link between the teachings of Aristotle, Galen, Euclid and Plato and the thinking of the modern Europeans."[2]

The achievements of medieval Arab/Muslim scholarship are firmly ensconced in the contemporary Arab psyche as manifestations of the vast intellectual superiority attained by their forefathers over an undistinguished West. Indeed, in some instances this concept of intellectual superiority was transmitted to contemporary Arabs by the medieval Islamic men of learning themselves. For example, as late as the fourteenth century when Arab civilization had already begun its gradual decline, the great North African philosopher of history Ibn Khaldun remarked: "We have heard of late that in the lands of the Franks, that is, the country of Rome and its dependencies on the northern shore of the Mediterranean, the philosophic sciences flourish . . . and their students are plentiful. But God knows best what goes on in those parts."[3]

While the medieval Arab men of learning could justifiably have used these contemptuous terms three or even two centuries earlier, by the fourteenth century the intellectual, as well as the political and military, balance of power had tilted so rapidly in favor of the West that any talk of Arab/Islamic superiority was hopelessly out of date. Indeed, from around the fifteenth century, the Arab world began a seemingly endless journey into oblivion. When, five hundred years later, the Arabs began to stir from their deep slumber, they awoke into a world that was no longer theirs; a nineteenth century world that was dominated politically, militarily and intellectually by Europe. That was the established order of the time, and there was little that the Arabs could do to undermine, or even compete with, it.

This sense of inferiority was nurtured by the Europeans' clearly articulated awareness of their own supremacy over the Arabs. Thus, for example, Sir Samuel Baker wrote of Colonel Ahmad Urabi who had led the revolt against British and French political and financial domination of Egypt, and who for his pains had suffered a crushing military defeat at the hands of the British in 1882: "He [Urabi] stirred up the latent fanaticism of his co-religionists by inciting them against the Christians. . . . Here was 'young Egypt' in the flesh, burning with enthusiasm, determined to show the world that Urabi was an incarnation of a great principle. . . . At the prick of the bayonet the bubble burst; and the ass in the lion skin galloped across the desert in cowardly flight."[4] The passage is indicative of European attitudes: not only was Urabi, a man who had become a national hero in Egypt, a fanatical bigot, but he was a stupid and cowardly one at that.

On the intellectual level, too, the Europeans reveled in the superiority of their cultural order, based on reason and science, contrasting it with the contemporary Arab situation, allegedly caught up in the dead-end of retrogressive Islam. Thus, for example, a leading French orientalist, Ernest Renan, asserted in a public lecture in 1880 that anyone could see the actual inferiority of the Muslim countries, the decadence of states governed by Islam, and the intellectual vacuity of the races adhering to Islam. He went on to condemn Islam as a religion incompatible with science and with new ideas.[5] And Renan was hardly alone among nineteenth-century European orientalists in contemptuously dismissing the Arabs and their religion as not only irrelevant to the present, but, because of the backwardness and rigidity of the religion, even more irrelevant for the future of humanity and its progress.[6]

It is true that during this period the half of the Arab world residing in Southwest Asia was languishing under the dominance of the fellow-Muslim Ottoman Empire. But by then the Ottoman Empire had long been the sick man of Europe, itself hostage to the will and whims of the Europeans. Indeed, with the final collapse of the Ottoman Empire after World War I and the division of the Asian Arab world into British and French spheres of influence, almost all of the Arab regions, in most cases independently of each other, were involved in a struggle to gain political independence from European domination.

The roots of contemporary Arab radicalism are lodged in that period spanning the second half of the nineteenth century and the first half of the twentieth when, in the perceptions of today's radicals, the Arabs rose against the established order, exemplified by a colonial and imperial Europe. Radicalism then was another term for anti-Westernism, and unlike the early Islamic period, anti-Westernism was born not of contempt for an inferior social order, but of the intense fear of a dominant civilization on the march, threatening to sweep the Arabs, their culture and religion into historical oblivion.

With time, the absorption of Western ideas into Muslim society, aimed initially at regenerating the stagnant Arab world, began to change in subtle ways the intellectual basis of the political struggle. European ideas of secular nationalism, espoused primarily by intellectuals of the Levant, began to compete with the more traditional Islamic emphasis. The divide was subtle but crucial. The Muslim radical thinkers and activists looked into their past and saw a religion that carried the Arabs to towering heights. The secularist radicals conceded the role of Islam, but saw its Arab essence as the primary motivating spark. Whatever their orientation, Arabs generally seemed united in their mistrust of, and hostility toward, the dominant European order, exemplified then by the two foremost imperial powers, Britain and France.

The immense Arab hostility to the two European powers drew many Arab political leaders and intellectuals of the nationalist and Islamic variety to Nazi Germany and Fascist Italy. Fully aware of the extent of British and French power, the Arabs saw their own salvation closely tied to, even contingent on, German and Italian victory over the allies. Beyond this, there was also an Arab fascination with a political and ideological system that seemed able in a short period of time to harness the talents and energies of the people and mobilize them into what appeared then to be an unstoppable force for progress and national primacy. Nazi Germany was indeed a monster, but its malevolence in the prewar period was confined primarily to Europe. The Arabs had not been touched by it. They were, on the other hand, tormented by the realization that, for all the facade of sovereignty and independence that some Arab countries possessed, they were not masters of their own destiny, but the objects of the political calculations and preferences of the real masters in London and Paris.

Arab torment was not destined to subside, since the Axis powers were defeated in World War II. But the war also undermined the dominance of Britain and France. The two European colonial powers emerged victorious but severely scarred, hardly able to protect interests abroad when so much needed to be done at home. The inherent weakness was not immediately apparent. The struggle against Communist domination in Malaya by the British and in Vietnam by the French sustained the facade of greatness and power, a facade that obscured the reality of an already collapsing imperial order. It was perhaps the Suez crisis in 1956 which spelled the end of the European era in Arab eyes. The two ailing great powers still had colonial possessions in the area, but by then the imperial bubble had already burst. Responsibility for maintaining the West's interests, or, more appositely in the eyes of the Arab radicals, the domination of the West, had already passed to the United States, a virtual newcomer to Middle Eastern and Arab politics and society.

The dawn of the American era occurred at a time when Arab hostility toward the West was rampant. Anti-Western sentiments at the popular level had reached a crescendo after the Arabs' defeat at the hands of the new state of Israel in 1948–49, because Israel was universally seen in the Arab world as a deliberate and conscious extension of "Western imperialism." Simultaneously, America's feverish efforts in the 1950s to press the various Arab countries into a Western-sponsored military alliance was interpreted as a veiled effort by the West to perpetuate its political and military domination of the area.

To counteract the established political order, that of Western political and military domination, the Arab radicals in the 1950s and 1960s resorted increasingly to the ideas and ideals of secular and nonaligned Arab nationalism. To Arab radicals in those decades, nationalism was the means by which a glorious past would be transformed into a heroic future. Through nationalism, with its obsession with ethnic heritage, Arabs drew courage from their long and distinguished history; through nationalism, with its emphasis on state-building, modernization and scientific development, the Arabs, for the first time in almost five hundred years, could become excited about their future. Yet this vehicle for material and intellectual advancement was being attacked, even humiliated and derided, by influential Western leaders, who persisted in interpreting the rising tide of nationalism as simply a masked Communist upsurge.[7]

In the radical interpretation of history, these attacks were essentially a continuation of the European onslaught on Islam and the Arab world since the late nineteenth century. Indeed, the situation at hand was even more serious, for in radical eyes, the West this time had been able to create, in Israel, a puppet in its own image, an extension of its expansionist self, of its own ideological and social order, and plant it in the midst of the Arab "nation," so that Western domination could be perpetuated. The relationship of tension and antagonism with regard to the West remained basically the same. Only the players had changed. Until World War II the imperial status quo meant Europe, particularly Britain and France, and it was primarily these two powers which took the brunt of Arab anger and hostility. Increasingly in the 1950s and 1960s it was the United States, directly and through Israel and its Arab "lackeys," which signified Western malevolent domination to the Arab radicals.

The picture was, of course, not as simple as this. There was always deep, but hidden, admiration for American scientific and intellectual achievements. American films particularly, depicting an advanced civilization and a vibrant social order buttressed by a seeming quality of life that was beyond even the most rampant imagination of any Arab, were obviously leaving their imprint on the Arabs' view of their world. Yet at the same time, this "show" of American cultural dominance, this apparent flaunting of the superiority of America's way of life, was seen by the radical Arab nationalists increasingly as an obscene case of "cultural imperialism." To be sure, the Arabs admired, even secretly envied, America's culture, but they also resented it and feared what it might do to their own social order.

In a sense, the combination of Arab admiration for, and fear of, the seductive American culture contributed to the vibrancy of the rising nationalist tide. The Arabs' admiration of America meant that they demanded a modern social order, emphasizing scientific and cultural advancements. The traditional elites were, therefore, increasingly seen in the context in which they presented themselves: status quo oriented, dependent for their survival on the dominant Western order. If the intention was to catch up with the West quickly in order to undermine its dominance, the Arab radicals became convinced that first they had to overthrow the traditional political leaderships. Moreover, to be able to satisfy quickly and effectively the demands of an *entire* society, when eyes had been opened to better things by exposure to a superior civilization, the emphasis had to be on an egalitarian political order in which the rewards would benefit the whole society. This awareness was of course far more acute in the relatively more advanced societies of Egypt and the Fertile Crescent. And in those countries "nationalism," "socialism" and rule by the "modernizing" military became the ideological trademarks of a radical generation which felt it was destined to deliver the Arabs and their lethargic world into a new heroic age of assertion and power. Spearheading the translation of dreams into reality was Egypt and its young and charismatic military leader, Gamal Abd al-Nasser.

From the mid-1950s onward, it was Egypt, under Nasser's vigorous direction, that challenged the dominant Western, increasingly American, order. In an endless stream of fiery speeches and commentaries, Egyptian radio bombarded the Arab world throughout the 1950s and 1960s with nationalist rhetoric evoking anti-Western, particularly anti-American, sentiments. They reminded the Arabs time and again of their glorious past, their military achievements, and their rich culture. Thus, for example, when the British and French were forced to withdraw from Suez, the event was likened to the Arab/Muslim victory over the Crusaders.

Beyond the memory of the past, Egypt would promise a brilliant future based on the present "achievements" and "victories" of nationalism and socialism. Much of this was rhetoric of course, but people accepted, approved and encouraged it, for the stand against imperialism was as much language as it was concrete policies. To the applauding multitude, who had suffered the humiliation of colonial domination, hurling insults at the once invincible and powerful was as good as defeating them militarily or standing up to them intellectually. Why should they not dance in the streets deliriously when they heard the young radical leader of Arab nationalism publicly tell mighty America: "We shall cut the tongue of anyone who dares to insult us. . . . We do not tolerate pressure and we do not accept humiliation. We are a people whose dignity cannot be sacrificed."[8] These were the heady days of radical nationalism, the force with which the Arabs would recreate the splendor of their distant past, the vehicle by which they would erase the humiliations of the recent past. Nationalism would thus constitute, or so people believed, the morality whereby the ultimate triumph of the Arab social order over American political and cultural "imperialist designs" would be achieved.

There were times when a meeting of minds, a sharing of dreams, existed between Abd al-Nasser and the Arab people. Particularly during the second half of the 1950s, the radical creed seemed to permeate all levels of Arab society, breaking all barriers between regime and people, state and citizens.[9] Consider, for instance, the circumstances in 1955 of the eventual refusal of Jordan and Lebanon to join the Western-sponsored military alliance called the Baghdad Pact. Britain, backed by the United States, had tried to persuade Lebanon and Jordan to join the Pact; the Lebanese had responded positively, but had indicated that they would wait for the Jordanian decision first. The Jordanian Prime Minister, Huzah al-Majali, had already declared his intention to join, and a formal request for membership was handed to the British ambassador on November 16, 1955. In December, Sir Gerald Templer, the British Chief-of-Staff, arrived in Amman seemingly to discuss Baghdad Pact membership. Egypt immediately unleashed a ferocious verbal campaign against the Templer mission, and throughout his visit, the Hashemite kingdom witnessed a wave of strikes, demonstrations and riots that were instrumental in bringing two governments down. The Templer mission failed, and both Jordan and Lebanon, having had their eyes opened to the power of the radical bond that tied the Arab masses to Nasser, shied away from the Pact.

This is but one of many cases in the second half of the 1950s in which Nasser's fiery radicalism fed the intense anti-colonialist and anti-imperialist orientation of the people. The coincidence of the two phenomena produced perhaps the only true radical mass movement of contemporary Arab history. To be sure, the glitter of Nasser's charismatic leadership began to fade and the adulation of the masses to subside in the early 1960s after the breakup of the United Arab Republic (of Egypt and Syria) and Egypt's ill-fated involvement in the Yemeni civil war. But, although less intense, the charismatic, symbiotic relationship endured. Even in his weakest moments, Nasser continued to dominate the Arab political landscape, and other Arab leaders had sleepless nights for fear of what Nasser's hold on their people might do to them and to their vulnerable political orders.

Radicalized by their interpretation of their history, their faith in Nasser's nationalist revolution, and their almost fatalistic hopes in an inevitable sparkling future, the pre-1967 Arab populations could intellectually accept the radical tenets of the thesis of "state and revolution." This thesis, enunciated by Egypt's political leaders in 1961 at the height of Egypt's radical march, draws a distinction between

> Egypt as a state and as a revolution. . . . If as a state Egypt recognizes boundaries in its dealings with governments, Egypt as a revolution should never hesitate or halt before these boundaries but should carry its message beyond the borders to the people in order to initiate its revolutionary mission.[10]

It was the general acceptance of this thesis that allowed Egypt and its President not only to carry out the country's radical policies, but also, and more importantly, to do that with popular approval of, or at least acquiescence in, the notion of Egypt's dual roles as state and as revolution.

But then Arab nationalism met its Waterloo in the June 1967 Arab-Israeli War. On the crucial issue of Palestinian rights Arab nationalism failed ignominiously, and with the failure sank the hopes and aspirations of the nationalist generation. After a whole decade of nationalist rhetoric and radical politics, the Arabs had gone to war against the "Zionist entity," confident of their inevitable victory under the banner of Arab nationalism, only to suffer the most humiliating defeat of their contemporary history. In the shocked aftermath the Arab situation began to be gradually transformed, for there can be little doubt that the June 1967 war was the watershed for popular radicalism.

Popular acceptance of a state's dual roles diminished swiftly and markedly. The war was a dramatic exhibition of the bankruptcy of the tenets of the "Arab revolution" proclaimed by Egypt and its radical leaders. Many began to argue that a revolution, with all the weight of its ideals, with all the moral and material resources it absorbed, was perhaps too heavy an albatross for a state to carry. And their conclusion was that Egypt and the Arab world might have been better served had Egypt's radical leaders concentrated more resources on the home front and less to the service of an anti-Western, anti-conservative, revolutionary march.

Just as crucial to the change in attitudes was a change in Egypt's own behavior from a pre-1967 regionally confrontational position to a policy of co-existence in the war's aftermath. Three related factors brought this about: First, the presence of Israeli soldiers on Egyptian soil made the goal of "Arab revolution" take a distinct second place to Egypt's primary postwar objective of "eradicating the consequences of aggression." Second, war-induced economic problems severely limited Egypt's developmental capabilities, imposing on Nasser an Egyptian rather than an Arab orientation. Third, as a consequence, Egypt's economic well-being very quickly became dependent on the financial assistance of the oil-rich but conservative and pro-Western Arab states, the very states against which Nasser's radical policies were directed. Thus it was only natural that once the high priest of revolution abandoned his radical mission, the flock would follow the lead and begin to see the role of the state in a more traditional sense, devoid of its revolutionary trappings.

Since then, there has not been, nor does it seem likely that there will be, a state or a political leadership in the Arab world that could credibly act as the focal point of an Arab mass movement and the repository of a whole peoples' political and social aspirations. The 1970s seem to have set the seal on the notion of the "revolutionary state of the masses." Instead, the rift between state and revolution in the Arab world has grown, with states exhibiting increasing confidence in their impregnability, their *raison d'être*, their ability to fight against hostile revolutionary groups and destroy them. The radicalism of Arab states in the 1970s, as it has been manifested in their relations with each other and with Israel and the West, has more to do with notions of power, prestige, and ranking in the Arab state system, as well as with the regimes' assessments of their own credibility, legitimacy and chances of survival, than with an ideological desire to be the vanguard of a mass revolutionary movement.

This is not to say that today's leaders do not believe in the ideals of the past, or that they do not use and exploit the symbolism of Arabism and Islam as instruments of their radical foreign policies. Nor do I mean to give the impression that the radicalism of Nasser's Egypt of the pre-1967 period was indifferent to considerations of power, political domination and personal aggrandizement. It is simply that the intense radicalizing environment of that period in Arab contemporary history, particularly the 1950s when the anti-imperialist struggle dominated the attitudes of masses as well as leaders, no longer permeated the consciousness, and consequently the behavior, of Arab states after 1967.

The ideals of the "revolutionary march of the masses" were transferred, after the debacle of the June 1967 war, to groups and movements which operated within states but which could count on, and boast of, allegiances across political borders and ideological frontiers. And increasingly in the 1970s and 1980s, these groups mounted a challenge to the sovereignty and integrity of the states. Their challenges were directed not only against conservative, status quo regimes, but also at so-called radical, even revolutionary leaderships. The radical movements which represented the main threat to state power in the 1970s have been the Palestinian guerrillas and the various Islamic organizations. In the next four chapters, I shall discuss the bases, motivations and performance of radicalism as manifested by the Arab states, by the Palestinians and by the Islamic groups.

Part Two

The Radical
Arab States

3
Their Institutions and Motivations

Every Arab regime, radical or non-radical, needs to be under-pinned by the indispensable organizational imperatives of social and political institutions. It is through these institutions that a regime can, on the one hand, respond more effectively to people's concerns, and on the other hand organize, even try to control, the country's social and political agenda. By its very nature, the radical regime tends to focus on societal mobilization. Dependence on institutions and organizations, which are encouraged to penetrate as many levels of society as possible, thus becomes a prerequisite for the regime's internal credibility, even for its stability. While the radical regimes have depended on socially and ideologically diverse kinds of institutions, their purpose and use are fundamentally the same: namely, preserve the regime in power by rendering it organizational support as well as ideological legitimacy; facilitate the successful implementation of the regime's radical policies; and to a lesser extent make an input to the decision-making process.

The core institutional unit in the Syrian and Iraqi political systems is the Baath Party. The 1971 Iraqi National Action Charter and the 1973 Syrian Constitution both depict the party as the "leading party in the state,"[1] prescribing a "democratic, revolutionary and unitary system."[2] Although in both states the Baath Party is supposed to share power with other "progressive" organizations and parties grouped under the banner of the Progressive National Front, in reality, the Baath Party remains the central, even the only, authoritative institutional organ.

While much antagonism permeates relations between the Baath Party's two wings in Damascus and Baghdad, there is very little variance in ideological commitment. Both wings of the party believe in the ultimate goal of Arab unity; both believe that the primary method of achieving this goal is through armed struggle; and consequently both publicly adhere to the concept of "revolutionary changes in Arab countries." While objective political and economic conditions may have intermittently heightened or diluted the commitments of party adherents to these revolutionary goals in the past, the fundamental radical principles of Baathism remain unchanged.

The National Liberation Front (NLF) in South Yemen and the Front de Liberation Nationale (FLN) in Algeria have been the primary political institutional units, both dedicated to radical and revolutionary principles. The Algerian FLN was born in 1954 with the beginning of the Algerian war of independence against the French. Similarly, the South Yemen NLF was one of two major political organizations that led the struggle for independence from British colonial control. Like the Baath Party in Iraq and Syria, the prominent positions of the FLN in Algeria and of the NLF—which was transformed in 1978 into the Marxist-Leninist Yemeni Socialist Party (YSP)—in South Yemen are due in no small part to their recognized status as parties and organizations that not only predated the establishment of the state, but actually founded it. As such, in neither state have other parties been allowed to intrude into the single-party system. And like the Baath, the Algerian and South Yemeni single-party organizations have been publicly committed to radical domestic and foreign policies born of their long anticolonial experience.

Libya's political institutions are also wholeheartedly committed to a revolutionary ideology. There is, however, an important departure from the model presented thus far. Far from creating, or even predating, the state, Libya's political organizations, as represented by the Arab Socialist Union (ASU) until 1976 and by the various popular congresses and committees thereafter, were themselves the creation of Libya's leader, Muamar Qadhafi. Lacking the prestige of an established party (e.g., the FLN) or of the source of ideological inspiration (e.g., the YSP) or of both (e.g., the Baath in Syria and Iraq), the ASU and the committees in Libya have had negligible influence on the regime's policies.

I do not suggest that the leaders of Syria, Algeria, Iraq and South Yemen are the prisoners of their parties' ideologies or political dictates. Far from it, for although these parties are indeed influential, their influence, with the possible exception of the YSP, is wielded within strictly imposed parameters in an Arab world that seems to be as vulnerable today as it was in earlier decades to the phenomenon of personalized leadership. Accordingly, it is not so much the party itself, even one with established status and prestige, but the key person within the party who tends to set the country's political orientation. Indeed, established parties do place certain limitations on the leaders' freedom of maneuver. But political power, and even in certain cases ideological direction, in the Arab world continue to reside with the chief executive, the man at the top of the political pyramid; for to set limitations is not to formulate or reverse policies, and to argue a point is not to make the argument stick.

This personal exercise of power is particularly the case in radical states for a number of reasons. First, a radical foreign policy geared more toward conflict than compromise necessitates the centralization of authority and the ability to circumvent institutional and bureaucratic procedures. Second, most radical leaders have come to power through military coups; and those who did not almost inevitably encountered active opposition from competitors who had little regard for the legitimacy of the succession process. Imbued with a conspiratorial ethic, radical leaders are bound instinctively to trust no one, and consequently to amass power in their hands and person. Third, conservative, status quo leaders, particularly monarchs, have at their disposal traditional symbols of legitimacy (e.g., tribal allegiances, religious prerequisites) and clearly defined lines of political succession, which makes it less necessary for the leader/monarch to circumvent established institutions and hustle for the direct support and attention of the people. Lacking traditional legitimacy, the radical leader is forever endeavoring to mobilize, and to establish direct ties with, his people, and in the process he undermines the role of state institutions. Direct communication with the masses was of course the domain of Abd al-Nasser in the 1950s and 1960s, a practice he perfected during the attack on Egypt in 1956 by Britain, France and Israel, when he addressed the Egyptian people from the pulpit of the famous al-Azhar Mosque in the tradition of the old caliphs who combined undisputed religious and political authority.[3] Such personal and direct efforts at mobilization have been emulated, perhaps less successfully, by all the radical leaders, particularly in times of crisis brought on by radical policies.

The personalization of political power in the radical Arab states is due also to certain social and cultural features relevant to radical and non-radical Arab states alike. These features seem to make the Arab people at least somewhat susceptible to centralized and authoritarian regimes. Socially, the core societal units in the Arab world have always been, and often still are, the tribe, the village, and the extended family. For centuries the pattern of political loyalty in the tribal and village communities was hierarchical, with authority focused on the *sheikh* or *rais*. Although bound by tribal and village laws and customs, the sheikh or the rais, assisted by elders and religious personages, acted as the central authority, final arbiter of power and ultimate dispenser of justice. Similarly, the extended family has traditionally been hierarchically structured with authority resting securely in the hands of the oldest member. Deference to, and respect for, family elders creates a far greater conformity within an Arab family than is usually the case in a Western family with its less hierarchical relationships. Transferred to the national milieu, therefore, the respectful and ready acceptance, in a tribal, village or family context, of a hierarchical social structure with a clearly identifiable authoritative person at the top obviously lessens rebellious popular tendencies against authoritarian regimes.

Equally crucial is the role of Islam. As the religion of the overwhelming majority of the Arab people, Islam pervades social custom and intrudes into cultural and political attitudes. To this day, many of the values, norms of behavior and attitudinal orientations of the Arab populations emanate from the inspiration and moral teachings of Islam. Moreover, Islam, recognizing no separation between state and religion, represents for many Muslim Arabs much more than just a system of spiritual guidance; it is accepted as a comprehensive social, political, legal and cultural system. Even after years of modernization and secularization, Islam remains a significant political force in the Arab world.

The normative imperatives of Islam bestow legitimacy on the centralized structure of political authority in the Arab world. The first major decision that the Muslim community had to make on the death of the Prophet Muhammad was the election of the first *Khalifa* (successor). The *Khalifa* was given religious and political authority, a decision based on the Sunna (the traditions of the Prophet) that religious and temporal power are inseparable. Moreover, centralization of authority is embodied in the Islamic political heritage through the pronouncements of many renowned Muslim jurists, theologians and philosophers in the centuries following the death of the Prophet. Thus, according to the fourteenth century philosopher of history, Ibn Khaldun, "it is in the nature of states that authority becomes concentrated in one person."[4]

These same jurists prescribed almost total obedience to the ruler by fostering the belief that "rebellion was the most heinous of crimes," a doctrine which "came to be consecrated in the juristic maxim, 'sixty years of tyranny are better than one hour of civil strife.'"[5] Thus, the renowned eleventh-century theologian al-Ghazali teaches that "an unjust ruler should not be deposed if strife would follow."[6] It is true that some jurists, such as al-Mawardi (d. 1058), argued that if the ruler did not fulfill his function, he should be removed from power, but none could indicate how this could be done legally or constitutionally. Other jurists, like al-Ash'ari (d. 935), "not only denied any right of popular revolution, but also emphasized the Caliph's full claim to obedience even if he had disregarded or violated his duties."[7] These and other similar theological views have constituted prescriptive knowledge embodied in the culture and heritage of the Arab/Muslim people, and so are bound to have had an impact on the way contemporary Arab populations tend to view authority.

The authoritarian radical leaders, however, cannot entrust the survival of their political orders to the force of tradition, or to their oratorical powers. Almost invariably, therefore, the radical leaders have created parallel pillars of support that stand alongside, and in competition with, the political institutions. Some have depended on family and clan support; some have drawn on narrow, yet fierce, sectarian loyalties; some have elicited the backing of military commanders and security chiefs; some have singled out a crucial segment of the existing political institutions (an active cadre) as the primary constituency of organizational support. And all have consistently used the mechanisms of state coercion to fill any remaining loopholes in the prevailing orthodoxy. Here contemporary radical leaders have been especially effective, since technology has placed in their hands methods of social and coercive suppression that have made earlier means of controlling the population pale into insignificance.

For all these reasons, therefore, the power to make decisions and enact policies in all the radical Arab states tends to be the domain of the man at the top; he dominates the decision-making process and determines the country's policy orientation. Indeed, one can go so far as to say that unlike Western democracies, where the chief executive derives his authority from the legitimacy of the political system, Arab political theory and practice have tended to elevate the leader, particularly in radical states, to a position of dominance over state institutions, thus making the legitimacy, even survival, of the political system a function of the ruler's credibility.

In this relationship the party perceives itself, and accordingly acts, as a decidedly subordinate institution to the presidency. For example, it took President Assad no time at all after assuming power in 1970 to dominate not only the Syrian Baath Party, but almost every aspect of Syria's decision-making process. Thus, a high-ranking member of the party confirmed that in meetings with the top membership of the Baath, Assad was the overriding personality, and his was the final decision on any policy.[8] Consider, moreover the deliberations of the ninth Regional Congress of Iraq's Baath Party, submitted in June 1982, at a time when Iraq's military efforts against Iran, which were closely identified with the leadership and policies of President Saddam Hussein, were going very badly. Not only was the Congress ecstatic about Iraq's achievements under Hussein, but it attributed to the President every success and exonerated him from any failure. The final report contained much praise, most of it directed to the personage of the chief executive. The Congress praised the ethical leading role of Comrade Leader Saddam Hussein in rebuilding the Party . . . praised his historic success in leading the Party . . . praised his decisive and historic role in planning and implementing the revolution . . . praised his distinguished ability and immense courage in confronting the conspiracies against the revolution . . . praised his rare ability to plan, devise and implement all the Party's prominent successes . . . praised his creative leadership in designing and implementing the economic development plan . . . praised his leading role in the war—in all its military, strategic, mobilizational, political, economic and psychological aspects—in a creative, courageous and democratic manner.[9]

In Libya, every political institution has found itself held hostage to the restless soul of the country's sole leader, Colonel Muamar Qadhafi. The first round of institutions centered on the Arab Socialist Union, established by Qadhafi on the Nasserite model. Frustrated by its inability to "educate and mobilize the masses," Qadhafi abolished the Union, and in a series of institutional and ideological reorganizations that spanned the years 1973–77 he created a revolutionary state in his own image. Instead of the single party, popular committees would supervise and make policy for localities and send delegates to the annual general meeting of the General People's Council (GPC), which would deliberate national policy.

Through this system, power is supposed to be entrusted into the hands of the people, and Qadhafi, who voluntarily relinquished all his formal positions as part of the institutional reorganization, would in theory observe the progress of the revolutionary march. Reality, however, is very distant from the ideals of theory. The "leader of the revolution" has in fact assigned himself the mission of ensuring that *his* revolution is not subverted by the "reactionary "tendencies that persist among some of Libya's population. Qadhafi has thus styled himself as the "leader of the opposition" in what essentially is his own political system. He will oppose "anybody who does not do his utmost to practice popular power." And the means of such opposition are to be found in his leadership of the revolutionary committees "whose task is to realize the era of the masses."[10] In reality, these committees are small groups totaling about 4,000 fully-fledged devotees of Qadhafi and his revolution, whose role it is to ensure the maintenance of popular enthusiasm for the regime. They fulfill this task internally and abroad by resort-

ing to a variety of more or less unsavory methods, such as liquida-
ting the enemies of the revolution. For all his public commitment to
the rule of the masses and the authority of the GPC, for nearly two
decades, Colonel Qadhafi continued to maintain a near monopoly
of the levers of political power in Libya.

Less theatrical but no less real is the dominance of the chief
executive over the party in Algeria. With all the FLN's prestige as
the organizational and symbolic focus of Algeria's war of independence, it did not take long for leaders to emerge who dwarfed the
FLN's political role in Algeria. Very quickly after independence, the
first constitution consolidated the role of the president as both head
of state and government and commander of the armed forces.

When Colonel Houari Boumedienne seized power in a military
coup in 1965, he immediately set about weakening the FLN by
abolishing the hitherto all-powerful Political Bureau and replacing
it with the National Council, which was staffed by Boumedienne's
supporters, many of whom, like him, were military commanders.
The Council became the real policy-making body. The president's
reorganization of the political system in 1976 did not change the
characteristics of power distribution. As the only nominated candi-
date, Boumedienne was elected president in December 1976 by 95.8
percent of the registered electorate. Until his death two years later,
he had no use for a vice president and continued to hold the
portfolios of the prime ministership and the ministry of defense.

Although the FLN tried to curtail the powers of the president
after Boumedienne's death, it soon became clear that the new in-
cumbent, Colonel Chadli Benjadid, would regain much of his predecessor's dominance of the FLN. The president retained the
pivotal role of the FLN's secretary general, and a decree in 1979 defined the functions of the prime minister as simply "helping" the
president with his governmental duties. Even the prime minister's
"organizational" powers were to be "delegated to him by the President."[11] In 1980 the president, as the FLN's secretary general, was
empowered to select the members of the party's resurrected Political Bureau rather than merely to propose them, and he was also
given a free hand in making other changes in the party which he
considered necessary. In July 1981 Benjadid removed from the
bureau Mohammed Yahiaoui and Abdelaziz Bouteflika, his main ri-
vals for the presidency in 1979. Later the hapless Bouteflika, along

with three other remaining party members who had held important portfolios under Boumedienne, was dismissed from the central committee. By 1983 Benjadid had established for himself unquestionable political primacy in the country and clear and pervasive domination over the party.

Leaders' primacy over the party is much more circumspect in South Yemen. It is difficult to ascertain why this should be the case. Perhaps it is because the NLF and later the YSP gradually developed a distinct Marxist-Leninist ideology and organizational structure, which elicited Soviet interest in promoting and protecting the party. Before he was ousted in January 1986, there were indications that President Ali Nasser was gradually moving toward a position of dominance over the YSP. After coming to power in 1980 until a few months before his removal from office, Nasser concentrated in his own hands the country's three most sensitive political positions—the presidency, the prime ministership and the party secretariat. He thereby felt able to embark on a course of rapprochement with the conservative Arab states. Nasser, however, was careful to rationalize his pragmatic foreign policy by referring to the Soviet Union's growing power worldwide, which allegedly had allowed socialist countries, like South Yemen, to engage in "peaceful coexistence" with capitalist countries from a position of strength.[12]

Ali Nasser's efforts to explain his policy orientation attested to the strength of the YSP and, beyond that, to the menacing shadow of the Soviet Union. South Yemen is a fragmented society in which power is atomized, and even the Islamic structure is very localized. Only the party seems to maintain a nationwide structure. Thus, unlike Algeria, where Benjadid's coterie of military commanders dominates the FLN, South Yemen's YSP completely controls the military. Party control extends far down the ranks, providing a key ideological input. Nasser should have remembered that the moderate policies of President Rubbayyi Ali precipitated the crisis within the NLF that led to Ali's ouster and the transformation of the NLF into the YSP. And indeed by 1984 the party was already becoming impatient with Nasser, who seems to have been accused of "being impotent from an ideological point of view to lead the political ideology of the party."[13] Such threats, perhaps abetted by the Soviets, should have been taken seriously by Nasser. But it seems that he did not. And the party in a bloody coup removed him from power, accusing him of trying to establish a dictatorial regime. Nasser's successor, Haidar Attas, and whoever may succeed him, may have learned the obvious lesson: that unlike other radical Arab parties, the Marxist-Leninist YSP continues to be a formidable counterbalance to the power of the president.

The centrality of the other radical Arab leaders in the decision-making processes of their countries does not mean that they are free of constraints in formulating and implementing policies and that political institutions act simply as rubber stamps for these policies, having relinquished their duty to probe and criticize. Although the parties' input into decision-making on a consistent basis is limited, they generally do set ideological bounds that leaders ignore at their peril. Moreover, cognizant of the party's role as an effective mobilizational support base, leaders have tended to go out of their way in pampering, consulting and deferring to the party, particularly in times of domestic or foreign policy crisis. Indeed, if there is one common trait among radical leaders, it is in the consistent way they endeavor to portray themselves as loyal party cadres and their policies as manifestations of party principles and goals. Consequently the relationship between party and leader in the Arab radical states is almost symbiotic: The president's power and authority are enhanced by the party's ideology and its organizational responsibilities within the country, and the party's status and influence are aided by the population's acceptance of presidential authority. It nevertheless remains the case in any power equation pertaining to the Arab radical states (except, perhaps, for South Yemen where the relationship is somewhat fuzzier) that the phenomenon of personalized leadership seems to be the dominant and key political variable.

Motivations

While it is true, as I argued in the preceding chapter, that the intense revolutionary environment of the 1950s, when the anti-imperialist struggle dominated the attitudes of the masses as well as their leaders, no longer characterized the more tranquil and low-key 1970s, it would be wrong to conclude that contemporary Arabs and their leaders are fired by no causes, moved by no ideals, or swayed by no ideologies. There are indeed other motivations for today's leaders to espouse Arab radicalism. These relate to personal and political considerations that have little to do with "revolutionary idealism"—considerations that, I concede, seem to be more important and pivotal than ideological beliefs and moral causes as the basis for policies. But that hardly means that Arabs, people and leaders alike, have lost the capacity to believe in "higher" things, that the common currency in the contemporary, materialistic Arab world is money rather than ideals, that an entire people have become a nation of "super-cynics."

This in fact, and interestingly, happens to be the argument increasingly propounded by some Western, especially American, specialists on the Middle East. Granted, most of those who write and comment on the Arab world accept that Arab leaders are constantly invoking ideological symbols, particularly those of Arabism and Islam, as primary justifications for their policies. Many analysts, particularly here in the United States, however, go beyond this and argue that these symbols are no more than just empty slogans used merely for public consumption. As such, Arabism and Islam and other ideological symbols are completely irrelevant as motivations for policy—a classic illustration of the "super-cynic" argument.

Let us consider the logic of this argument. If the invocation of ideals and ideological symbols by leaders of the Arab radical states does not represent their true beliefs but is merely for public consumption, then this presupposes *a fortiori* the prevalence of these ideals and symbols as important social values, at least to crucial segments of that society. Otherwise, what benefit would accrue to the leaders from the use of the symbols? Since leaders need societal support to perpetuate their rule, then these values must in some way motivate policies, for nowhere could people be so utterly and so consistently deceived.

Yet, this reasoning could be negated by the argument that the intense authoritarianism of the Arab radical regimes precludes the necessity for dependence on public support, that Arab radical leaders rule through oppression and coercion and hence have no overwhelming desire to seek public support that might well entail some relaxation of their total political control. If we are to accept such an argument (and I can think of few more inane arguments), then the invocation of ideological symbols by the radical (and also by "moderate") Arab leaders, even for public consumption, becomes redundant. The only other explanation for the constant public invocation of these symbols by the leaders could be that the values in question constitute their *personal* principles. Either way, it seems to me grossly simplistic to argue that the deep-seated values of Arabism and Islam are constantly being cynically manipulated by leaders who do not believe in them and that such values have no motivational role in the formulation of policies.

One motivating impulse for radical politics, therefore, is a leader's belief in radical ideology. In no case in the Arab world is this the only motivation for radicalism; indeed, in no case (with the possible exception of South Yemen) is it the most significant factor; but, equally true, in no case is it without validity. All of today's radical Arab leaders lived their formative years during the political upheavals of the anti-imperialist era. Indeed, the Algerian and South Yemeni leaders during the 1970s and 1980s were themselves active in the struggle against French and British colonialism in the 1950s and 1960s. Physically living through the long years of revolutionary experience, with all its hardships and all its triumphs, has surely made a deep impact on the way these leaders view their world.

Less obvious, but still relevant to my case are the experiences of the leaders of Libya, Syria and Iraq. Qadhafi's formative years coincided with the height of Abd al-Nasser's nationalist onslaught in the mid and late 1950s. In a 1983 interview, Qadhafi described Abd al-Nasser as "the hero of the Arab nation. . . . He was a powerful opponent of colonialism, and he was loved by the ordinary masses, the simple masses. He expressed what was within us, our feelings and aspirations."[14] A school friend of Libya's president asserted that the basic ideas Qadhafi expounded in the political speeches he was making in 1960 at the age of 18 were identical with those he advocated after becoming head of state.[15]

The association of Syria's Assad and Iraq's Hussein with the Baath Party early in their lives also left its mark on their political consciousness. Each became an adherent of Baathist ideology in his early teens, and each was an active participant in the Baath's early struggle for political power in, respectively, Syria and Iraq. In 1959, when Saddam Hussein was in his early twenties, he participated in a Baathist plot to assassinate Iraq's ruler, Abd al-Karim Qassem, a man increasingly seen by the Baathists as a tool of the Communist Party. The assassination attempt failed, and Hussein was injured. He later confided in an interview that for all his "achievements later on in life, that was perhaps his most cherished memory."[16] For Hussein, as well as for Assad, serving Baathist revolutionary principles in their younger days could not but leave an imprint on later years. Obviously, once in power, these commitments to radical and revolutionary ideology had to be balanced against the objective, sometimes harsh, political, domestic, regional and international realities. And while these ideological commitments have not been completely compromised, certainly adherence to another principle—that of survival of the leader and his regime as well as the political order they stand for—has taken precedence over ideological purity.

To return to my earlier argument, the survival of leaders and their regimes ultimately depends on their responsiveness to the values and ideals of their population. In order to survive, the authoritarian radical leader, lacking the legitimacy based on political institutions, must project a capability to "deliver the goods." He must be seen by his populace, particularly by key segments, as a successful, meritorious and responsible leader. Needing to be unashamedly populist, the Arab radical leader must be sensitive to his people's cherished values. He can try to infuse his society with new values, but he cannot afford to find himself too far out of step with his people's predominant value system. He must work—or must appear to the populace to be working—to achieve the goals of that value system, and he must be seen as successful in achieving these goals. If not, his survival cannot be guaranteed.

In the first chapter, I argued that the major value system in the Arab world, which has formed a powerful ideological force cutting across state boundaries and has consistently influenced the policies and orientations of radical leaders, consists of the two values that have dominated the political consciousness of Arabs, namely, Arabism and Islam. Unlike the situation in any other region of the contemporary international system, these two values shape political attitudes throughout the region, flowing across geographic state boundaries. Arab leaders, thus, have perhaps less to fear from a military buildup in a neighboring Arab country than from a heightened popular perception of a neighboring leader as a successful defender of Arab and Islamic rights.

This is not to say, however, that the power of these two ideological forces is felt uniformly among the various Arab states. It is indeed true that the various components of the contemporary Arab world share a common heritage. But within this broad social and cultural unity, differing historical influences have made some Arab countries and their citizens more susceptible than others to the moral and ideological dictates of one or the other of the two values.

Egypt and Syria are cases in point. Whereas Egypt, even under Ottoman and British control, had always constituted, and had always been perceived as, a single identifiable social and political unit, Syria was more of an abstraction, divided as it was during the Ottoman period into a number of administrative units. Egyptians' emotional and political devotion to the concept of Egypt was consequently much stronger than Syrians' attachment to the notion of Syria. It was only natural, therefore, that the Syrians, without a powerful ideological force of self-identification, would more readily embrace the all-encompassing idea of radical Arab nationalism. The Egyptians, on the other hand, enamored almost to the point of obsession with their Egypt, found it difficult to subsume their Egyptian identity into a broader Arab identity. For instance, the term Arab was completely absent from the memorandum on "Egypt's national claims" which the Egyptian national leader, Saad Zaghloul, presented to the Geneva Peace Conference in 1919.

It is within this context that President Nasser of Egypt, who for an entire generation of Arabs had epitomized the moving spirit of Arab nationalism, told a Syrian delegation with astonishing frankness: "The national feeling in Syria has been clear for a long time. In Syria when an infant is born, he utters the words Arab nationalism and Arab unity. . . . Here in Egypt, the feeling emerged only in 1955 or 1956."[17] Reorienting Egyptian attitudes toward their Arab neighbors entailed a massive "educational" program in the 1950s and 1960s—almost an indoctrination campaign—an effort whose success to this day remains nebulous.

This is why Egypt, the leading radical Arab state in the 1950s and 1960s, could so easily revert in the 1970s to its dormant, yet powerful, Egyptianness. And this is how President Sadat, basing his legitimacy on an "Egypt First" policy, could do what he did with relative confidence: He could sign a separate peace treaty with Israel outside the Arab context; he could subscribe to a vague notion of Palestinian autonomy; and he could completely sidestep the emotional issue of East Jerusalem. Can anyone imagine the President of Syria—"the beating heart of Arabism"—ever contemplating, let alone pursuing, the same policy!

The attitude of the Egyptian leaders throughout their long negotiations with the Israelis during 1978–79 was that, while they would try to salvage what they could for their Arab and Palestinian "brothers," their main concern must be Egypt's national interest. To the radical Syrian leaders, dependent for their legitimacy on popular perception of them as *the* defenders of Arab rights, there could be no differentiation between Syria's national interest and the interests of the "Arab nation" as a whole. Thus, the Syrians have repeatedly argued—an argument which seems to have fallen on deaf ears in the West—that the return of the Golan Heights to Syrian sovereignty would not by itself modify Syria's hostility to Israel. Only the promise of a comprehensive redressing of Palestinian and Arab grievances against Israel would make Syria amenable to the idea of negotiations with the "enemy of the Arabs." Differing historical experiences thus explain why radical Arabist ideology has been more resilient in Syria than in Egypt.

Generally, however, and particularly among the radical Arab states, Arabism and Islam are potent destabilizing agents since they can be used by a leader in one Arab country to lay claim to the loyalty of the population of another. To be seen as acting against the interests of Arabism and Islam invites not only possible domestic unrest, but also the double danger of destabilization by a neighboring Arab and/or Islamic regime putting itself forward as an alternative leadership. Herein lies the utility of these symbols to the radical leader. The danger that Qadhafi of Libya seemed to have posed to the stability of the political order of Egypt's Anwar al-Sadat lay not in Libya's military might, but in Qadhafi's appeals to the Egyptian masses to compare his own Islamic and Arab commitments with those of Sadat.

President Saddam Hussein of Iraq felt so threatened by Ayatollah Khomeini's calls to the Iraqi population to overthrow the "non-Islamic, infidel rulers" of Baghdad that he went to war against those "using religion to foment sedition and division among the ranks of

the Arab nation."[18] The transnational Islamic magnetism was so
powerful that only through an invocation of Arab nationalist symbolism—an appeal to the "Arab" Iraqis to re-create the battle of
Qadissiya, when in 637 A.D. the Arabs defeated the Sassanid Persians—could the Iraqi leaders hope to neutralize Iran's undoubted
Islamic appeal. These instances demonstrate in microcosm the
broader context of regional politics in which Arabism and Islam
play a central role.

To follow radical policies that are designed, genuinely or ostensibly, to defend or enhance Arabism and/or Islam also serves to se-
cure the domestic credibility of radical leaders. Syria's policies toward Israel during and after the Israeli invasion of Lebanon in June
1982 provide an interesting illustration. As I argued in the first
chapter, "steadfastness" against Israeli policies in the region is an
essential feature of the radical creed in the Arab world. The manner
in which the Damascus regime presented Syria's steadfastness
against Israel in 1982–83, contrasting it with the "capitulationist attitudes" of other Arabs, clearly did much to enhance the stability of
the Assad regime. By the same token, policies that are projected as
defending Arab rights and/or Islamic ideals have been directed
against fellow Arab leaders and regimes. Again, whether genuine
or not, these policies clearly are used as a legitimating agent. I shall
analyze these arguments in more detail in the next chapter.

In addition to creating a supportive domestic environment, a
radical foreign policy has the immediate goal of promoting a regime's security. The creation of a more conducive regional environment through the weakening or overthrow of antagonistic or competitive regimes and their replacement with compatible and
friendly ones would minimize externally generated security
threats. In South Yemen, for example, the efforts undertaken by the
Marxist Aden government to undermine the stability of North
Yemen and the Gulf states, particularly the Sultanate of Muscat and
Oman and the Kingdom of Saudi Arabia, stem, at least in part, from
the fear of the "imperialist" designs of these pro-Western states,
which have harbored Yemeni emigres hostile to the radical South
Yemeni regime.

The bitter hostility that characterized relations between the
two Baathist regimes in Baghdad and Damascus is another case in
point. To the Iraqis, the Syrian regime was an "illegitimate entity

which has shamelessly trampled upon all Arab values and principles, and which will be swept out of power by the principled Arab people of Syria."[19] For their part, the Syrians were no less venomous. To them, the Baghdad government represented "a fascist regime of executions, blood and gallows; a regime drowning in isolation."[20] Similar to the Sino-Soviet conflict, Iraqi-Syrian enmity reflected generous doses of personal animosities and jealousies, as well as an acute ideological rivalry: which of the two leaderships should be seen by the Arab populace as the true representative of Baathist ideology, and which of the two capitals ought to be regarded as the center of the Arab radical movement. Legitimacy accorded to one would constitute a direct threat to the credibility, even survival, of the other.

Each regime's acute awareness of a competitive leadership that could employ the same ideological symbols to appeal to its population's loyalty explains their vehement and long hostility. In order to remove the competition, both regimes waged against each other an intense war of propaganda, subversion, and economic deprivation. Indeed, in one or two instances, they went to the brink by massing their armed forces on their common border. Throughout the 1970s and well into the 1980s the enmity between these two radical regimes has surpassed, in its virulence and its constancy, anything that had existed between radicals and moderates elsewhere in the Arab world. And in this struggle the two radical regimes assailed each other in the same terms that they had employed individually in their onslaught against moderate, pro-Western regimes—utilizing the broad themes of the defense of Arabism, the anti-imperialist struggle and the righteous crusade.

A radical orientation need not, however, constantly produce, in a deterministic fashion, violent and subversive policies. Indeed, in a number of cases, Arab radical leaders have responded to evolving domestic and international situations by adopting pragmatic, even moderate, policies. (I shall chronicle some of these policy changes in the next chapter.) However, since all these countries find it imperative to reassert their adherence to the radical principles of their founding parties and institutions, the adoption of pragmatic policies seems to be dictated by tactical considerations that relate to the leaders' evaluation of the best method of ensuring their perpetuation in power and improvement in status. If and

when moderation is assessed as having failed to achieve its required objective, it will certainly be discarded, and a return to
radicalism will be effected. For only when there is a fundamental
change in the world view of the radical Arab leaders and their
populations, entailing an attitudinal reorientation in the way they
perceive their role in the Arab system, the role of Israel in the wider
Middle Eastern system, and the role of the United States vis-à-vis
both systems, would a change toward a more moderate stance
be considered as anything more than a transient and tactical
phenomenon.

4

. . . And Their Activities

Role of ideol. + beliefs in det.
policies

Desire | Arab leaders to legit.
their rule

Soviet P.P._ + state
policies -

L ike all states, radical states conduct their foreign policies according to a variety of motivations. As outlined in the preceding chapter, these motivations normally relate to a set of beliefs, perceptions of state and personal interests, and assessments of the objective conditions operative at a particular time. In other words, in formulating and implementing their foreign policies, radical states do not differ in any appreciable way from other states in the international system. Radical states, thus, are not "crazy"—i.e., idiosyncratic and unpredictable entities, whose "wild" behavior tends to create havoc in the international system. They certainly differ from status quo countries in their beliefs, goals and ideologies and consequently may not conform to norms of behavior acceptable to a status quo international system. But that is not to say that their behavior defies analysis or comprehension, that there is no logic to their conduct, or that we can never understand them or their ways. Even if the results of their policies seem to us totally abhorrent, and even if their leaders and regimes to our Western sensibilities appear sinister, sometimes even deranged, the process by which decisions are made is analyzable, and the reasons for the decisions are comprehensible, if not always acceptable, to us.

In this chapter, I analyze radical politics thematically by highlighting the relationship between motivations and state policies. It goes without saying that motivations differ in impact and power from one radical state to another. Here lies an important consideration: radical states are separate entities, with different social and political conditions, and should not be lumped together, as is sometimes the habit in Western intellectual circles, into specific universal categories that are usually derogatory: e.g., "fanatical," "Soviet client," "uncivilized," etc. To be sure, there are certain analytical categories (e.g., Islam, personalized leadership, etc.) that run across the entire Arab radical spectrum, but their potency varies as they interact with the specific social and political conditions of each state. In identifying the various factors that motivate radical policies, I shall examine their potency by drawing on specific examples of state action to which these factors happened to be particularly relevant.

Let us consider the role of beliefs and ideologies in motivating radical policies. As noted in Chapter 3, it is almost impossible not to find traces of ideology in the policies of radical states. However, the influence of the ideological factor is not uniform; it varies not only from one state to another, but also within a state from one specific time period to another.

The avowedly leftist regime of South Yemen has been the one regime that has adhered consistently and publicly to a Marxist-Leninist ideology that sees everything in terms of class struggle. In this world view, progressive regimes are part of the "international proletarian solidarity" and thus are friends, whereas conservative states are considered part of the "imperialist," "capitalist" conspiracy and are by definition foes of Aden.

South Yemen policies in Arabian Peninsula and Gulf politics testify to Aden's ideological commitment. Throughout the 1970s, South Yemen actively supported dissident and revolutionary movements (e.g., Popular Front for the Liberation of Oman and the Arab Gulf (PFLOAG), the Saudi Communist Party, the dissident National Democratic Front (NDF) in North Yemen, etc.). The PFLOAG was a particular favorite, since it also was a vehement adherent to Marxist-Leninist precepts. Aden thus provided safe haven, arms, logistical support and training to the PFLOAG until its collapse in the mid-1970s. Another indication of the pre-eminence of Marxist ideology can be seen in the way Aden has viewed broader Arab concerns. Arab unity and identity, for instance, are considered South Yemeni goals but are conceived of as subordinate to "class interests."[1] Thus in the conflict between "Marxist" Ethiopia and "Arab" Somalia, Ethiopia has received consistent South Yemeni support. Similarly, important as the goal of Yemeni unification undoubtedly is, Aden has insisted that North Yemen must have a "progressive" political system before unity could occur. Although the two countries signed a series of unity protocols in 1982, these have not been put into operation because of the divergent ideological outlooks of the two regimes.

In the Arab-Israeli conflict, Israel is perceived in Aden as a Western outpost and an agent for American imperialism dedicated to the struggle against "progressive" forces, and therefore an obstacle to revolution in the region. South Yemen is thus a wholehearted supporter of the "Palestinian Revolution." It has provided the PLO with arms, it has sent "volunteers" to fight alongside the Palestinians in Lebanon, it has allowed Palestinian guerrillas to use South Yemen for training purposes. And it has been a faithful and militant advocate of Palestinian maximalist demands in the Arab world.

What is interesting from an ideological point of view is that, while Aden supports PLO unity, it has particularly close contacts with the more radical Marxist groups, such as the Popular Front for the Liberation of Palestine (PFLP), the Democratic Front for the Liberation of Palestine (DFLP), and the Palestinian Communist Party; accordingly, these groups are given disproportionate coverage in the South Yemeni media. Similarly, South Yemen was quick to grant diplomatic recognition to the Polisario, viewing it as a progressive national liberation movement struggling against the conservative and pro-American Moroccan government. That this view is influenced primarily by ideology can be surmised by Aden's treatment of the Eritrean liberation movement, which it condemns as separatist, because, contrary to the Moroccan case, it is acting against the "progressive" Ethiopian regime.

Aden's adherence to its ideology has not been totally uniform; yet, compared with other radical regimes, it has shown firm ideological commitment by word and deed. For example, in return for an end to Aden's active support for radical movements in the Arabian Peninsula, Saudi Arabia in 1978 promised $25 million for South Yemen's five-year development plan and over $100 million for other projects. Additionally, the Saudis offered to finance the

expansion of the oil refinery in Little Aden and to supply the necessary crude.[2] Since South Yemen is one of the poorest Arab countries
with hardly any natural resources, the Saudi rulers, accustomed to
successfully buying off other troublesome radical leaders, must
have been more than surprised when Aden ignored their benevo-
lence.

If not to this extent, ideological beliefs have nonetheless promi-
nently motivated the policies of other Arab radical regimes. President Qadhafi's commitment to Arab unity seems to supersede
other considerations. From early youth an ardent supporter of the
late President Nasser of Egypt, Qadhafi has long considered the organic unity of the Arab world essential to overcome its weaknesses
and sense of inferiority toward the West. This indeed must explain,
at least in part, Qadhafi's almost obsessive pursuit of unity schemes
with other Arab states since coming to power in 1969. He sought
unity in its various forms with Sudan, Syria and Egypt during 1970–
73; with Tunisia in 1974; with Syria, Mauritania and Algeria in 1980–
83; with Morocco in 1984; and in 1985 with Sudan.

It is obvious from this disparate array of Arab states that the
terms radical, revolutionary or progressive need not characterize a
state's ideological and political orientation for Qadhafi to covet
union with it. Indeed, prior to his unity overtures, Morocco and
Sudan had been the object of intense Libyan propaganda attacks
and subversive activities. And in Sudan's case, Qadhafi reportedly
offered ex-President Nimeiri $5 billion to bail out Sudan's besieged
economy in exchange for a Sudanese agreement to unite with
Libya.

Again, Libya's uncompromising stand against Israel and support for the militant Palestinian posture relates in part to Qadhafi's
and the Libyans' view of imperialism through their own experience
with Italian colonialism in Libya. Israel is seen as analogous to the
Italian settler colony in Libya, born of an excess European population and supported by Western interests, on a basis of alleged historical justification, and detrimental to the indigenous Arab population. Consequently, the Libyans, at odds even with the PLO and
other radical Arabs, do not accept the concept of a Palestinian state
in the West Bank, but advocate the complete eradication of "Zionist
imperialism" in Palestine.

Qadhafi's commitment to Islam meshes with his anti-imperialist views since, for him, Islam is a revolutionary movement struggling against global imperialism and its "lackeys" in the Middle East. Thus the Libyans provided cash for Khomeini's opposition to the Shah. Tripoli also arranged for financial and military transfers to Palestinian and leftist/Muslim groups in Lebanon, to the Polisario in the Western Sahara, to the Muslim opposition in Nigeria and the Philippines, as well as to the Irish Republican Army (IRA) and the Nicaraguan Sandinistas. Qadhafi has also allowed guerrillas and terrorist groups acting internationally against Western, particularly American, interests to use Libyan soil for training purposes.

Because of its own long and costly revolutionary past, Algeria too is committed to national liberation movements. However, the experience of its tortuous war of independence has taught it the imperative value of unity. This is clearly shown in Algeria's attitudes toward the PLO. For unlike South Yemen and Libya (as well as other Arab countries), Algeria refuses to sponsor or promote various Palestinian groups on the basis of their ideological outlooks. Accordingly, while its unbending support for the Palestinian struggle (which in a sense continues to revitalize "Algeria's revolutionary self-conception"[3]) has nurtured the Palestinian movement from the outset, Algeria has remained true to its emphasis on unity by refraining from intervening in the movement's internal affairs. For this reason, the Palestinians, faced with divisions and dissent after the PLO's expulsion from Beirut, decided to hold their Palestinian National Council (PNC) meeting in February 1983 in Algiers. Significantly, too, the Algerians refused to host the next PNC meeting (which eventually took place in Amman in November 1984) because Yasser Arafat had decided not to delay any longer in the hope that smaller pro-Syrian PLO factions would participate.

Nor should the influence of Baathist ideology on Syria's support for the Palestinian cause be minimized. The revolutionary character of Baathism, in addition to its nationalist obsession with the Arab "homeland," was *one* contributing factor (for indeed there were others, some probably more crucial, which I shall analyze later) to the Syrian commitment to the Palestinian cause that was once articulated by President Assad in these terms:

How much have we sacrificed for the Resistance in the past few years? Fifty percent of the Syrian military aircraft destroyed in clashes with the enemy [Israel] before the 1973 war were in the defense of the positions of the Palestinian Resistance. Thirteen planes were lost in only one day in Urqub in defense of the Resistance. These aircraft were manned by the elite of our pilots. . . . We lost 500 soldiers in one day. We lost them in a fight with the enemy because the enemy had hit a Fidai [guerrilla] base somewhere in Syria. The battles we fought against the enemy for the sake of the Palestinian Resistance are numerous. . . . Who has done for the Resistance what Syria has done? Who has sacrificed for the Resistance what Syria has sacrificed?[4]

These were no empty words, for while there have been periods of extreme tension and antagonism, particularly after the expulsion from Lebanon first of the PLO by the Israelis in 1982 and then of Arafat's loyalists by the Syrians themselves in 1983, the closeness of Syrian-Palestinian relations until 1982 was not duplicated anywhere else in the Arab world. Indeed, time and time again, the Palestinians themselves reiterated and emphasized throughout the 1970s Syria's role as the "defender of the Palestinian revolution." The only discordant note to this warm relationship in the 1970s occurred in the summer and autumn of 1976 when Syrian troops entered Lebanon to fight on the side of the rightist Christians against the leftist Muslim/Palestinian forces.

The reasons for this intervention were many, and I have enumerated them elsewhere.[5] One reason was that Syria's ideological commitment to the Palestinians was confronted and eventually superseded by another ideological concern, prompted by a perception that the continuation of hostilities by the Palestinians and their Muslim allies against the Christians would inevitably lead to the division of Lebanon. As committed believers in Arab unity (for example, Arab states are referred to in Syrian high school textbooks, in accord with Baathist terminology, as "regions" of the Arab homeland), the Baathist leaders were bound to resist vigorously any further "balkanization" of the Arab world, especially if this were to happen along religious lines, given Baathist adherence to secularism. Moreover, their ideological distrust of the West, and of the Western "puppet," Israel, heightened their fears that the division of Lebanon would serve no one's interest but that of the "Zionists" and the "imperialists." Apart from other considerations, Syria's offensive against the Palestinians in Lebanon in 1976 had, in the Syrian mind, a clear ideological rationale.

Militant Baathist ideals, as we have seen in the preceding chapter, were translated faithfully by the Iraqi regime into a concerted political offensive against the so-called reactionary Arab states. The first decade of the Iraqi Baathist leadership (1968–78) was seemingly dedicated to the fight against "feudalist" Arab "reactionaries," the "stooges of imperialism," particularly those close to the United States, such as the Kingdom of Saudi Arabia and the Gulf Sheikhdoms. In December 1972 an Iraqi road-building crew crossed the border into the neighboring Gulf state of Kuwait and, under the protection of an Iraqi military brigade, began to build a road leading to the Gulf in Kuwaiti territory. Later, in March 1973, Iraqi troops occupied a Kuwaiti police station at Samitha, an action which led to a number of Kuwaiti casualties. During this period, radical Iraq had very little respect for the sovereignty claims of what it regarded as reactionary entities. Up until the second half of the 1970s, the Iraqi leadership consciously endeavored in its rhetoric and behavior to emphasize that the ideological goal of the eradication of the reactionary enemies of the Arab nation constituted the mission, even the *raison d'être*, of the radical Baathist leadership.

More interesting were Iraqi efforts to explain in ideological terms the country's turn to moderation and pragmatism in the late 1970s and early 1980s, which culminated in Hussein's enunciation in February 1980 of the Arab National Charter. The Charter contained such principles as: "disputes among Arab states shall be resolved by peaceful means . . . with recourse to armed force prohibited"; "Arab states should reaffirm their adherence to international law . . . and should steer clear of the arena of international conflicts and wars"; and "Arab states should undertake to establish close economic ties among each other."[6]

This was indeed a far cry from the Baathist revolutionary creed of the early 1970s. But according to Iraqi leaders, the new pragmatism was dictated by emerging circumstances and was no less effective than earlier revolutionary policies in achieving Baathist values and goals. The Iraqi leaders argued that Egypt's withdrawal from the Arab-Israeli conflict as a result of the Camp David Accords in 1978, coupled with the emergence of a new threat against the "Arab nation" in the form of the violently expansionist Islamic republic in Iran in 1979, exposed the Arab world to new dangers which necessitated the adoption of new policies. Revolutionary policies seeking to undermine the stability of other Arab regimes would thus only serve to weaken the Arab world further, seriously and adversely affecting its ability to confront new, potentially mortal dangers. Pragamatism and moderation toward Arab states and strict adherence to the goal of Arab solidarity were, the Iraqis insisted, true manifestations of their continuing principled commitment to Baathist ideological strictures.

Iraq's attack on Iran in September 1980, aimed at overthrowing the Khomeini government, was in our terms of reference a manifestly radical act. Many reasons motivated Iraq's initiation of military hostilities; but Baghdad's constant emphasis on, even pride in, the Arabism and secularism of Iraq, which was indicative of the much broader Baathist system of values held by the leadership, inevitably would make the Iraqi leaders question the intentions of the "theocratic Persians." To President Hussein, therefore, the Iranian clergy were manipulating religious symbols "to foment sedition and division among the ranks of the Arab nation," and as "a mask to cover up Persian racism and a buried resentment against the Arabs."[7] Interpreting Iran's intentions and policies through an ideological prism may not have been the foremost catalyst for Iraq's invasion of Iran, but there is little doubt that it was a contributing factor.

As argued in Chapter 3, beyond ideology, another and possibly more important factor motivating the foreign policies of radical states is the constant efforts by Arab leaders to legitimize their rule and ensure their survival in the absence of legitimacy based on political institutions. This they would do by embarking on activities in domestic or foreign policy that would be expected to strike a responsive chord among the population. The image of the leader as a "meritorious" individual, acting with wisdom and/or courage on behalf of values and concerns dearly held by the population, would ultimately bestow on the leader the legitimacy needed to ensure his regime's survival. Thus leaders of radical states have sometimes embarked on activist, even aggressive, foreign policies in order to enhance their legitimacy at home.

I do not mean to suggest that Arab radical leaders are forever searching, even manufacturing, foreign ventures in order to legitimize their rule. Nevertheless, given the environment of Arab politics, it is easy to see why there is such a strong correlation between domestic legitimization and an activist foreign policy. Conflict in the the region is endemic: the perennial Arab-Israeli struggle; the territorial issues born of the colonial legacy, in some cases yet unresolved; and the many sectarian and ethnic divisions that cut across state boundaries, leading not only to intra-state but also to inter-state conflict. Finally, the citizens of the various Arab states tend to identify with the universalist values of Arabism and/or Islam. These values, as we have seen in the preceding chapter, not only work to weaken citizens' identification with their own states, but are also regularly used by Arab leaders to appeal to the loyalty of the citizens of other Arab states. Characterized by an intense level of inter-state activity, the Arab political environment has made foreign policy a most convenient vehicle for regime stability and legitimacy.

President Assad's activist policy in Lebanon in the post-June 1982 period is an interesting illustration. Syria's commitment of troops both in the air and on the ground against the advancing Israeli forces, although objectively a failure, was projected by the Syrian leadership as a measure of the sacrifices Syria was prepared to make on behalf of the "Arab nation." Damascus' subsequent tough stand against the May 1983 Israeli-Lebanon agreement, and the eventual vindication of its obstinacy, gave the Assad regime untold credit in both Syria and the Arab world among a people increasingly frustrated and humiliated by Israel's seemingly hegemonic power, especially since such pivotal Arab regimes as Egypt, Jordan, Iraq and Saudi Arabia had publicly or privately approved the agreement. Assad's status soared even higher when he refused to cave in under increasing American military pressure—a stand that led to Syria's shooting down of two American aircraft and capture of one pilot.

The prestige that accrued to Syria as a result of these activist and radical acts, which were projected as a brave defense of Arab rights, had crucial domestic manifestations for the Syrian regime. President Hafiz al-Assad and a number of key members of the Syrian leadership belong to the minority Alawi community. The Sunni Muslims, who constitute the vast majority of the Syrian population, have tended to be antipathetic toward the Alawi sect, an esoteric offshoot of Ismaili Shiism that seems to have absorbed animistic and Christian beliefs. This hostility is reinforced by a deep-rooted Sunni resentment of the recent Alawi political ascendancy—a resentment related not only to the minority status of the Alawi, but also to the Sunnis' long-standing contempt for their previously inferior material, social and educational standing.

Until the late 1970s the Baath Party constituted the main ideological base of the Assad regime in Syria. The President's consciously public adherence to the party's principles and his regime's advocacy of the Baath as the primary vehicle for upward mobility in Syria's political and economic systems blurred the regime's dependence on the Alawi community for its security. Thus, for example, General Rif'at al-Assad, the President's brother, and his praetorian guard, the Defense Companies (Siraya al-Difa'), generally endeavored to execute their security functions with some discretion, thereby allowing attention to focus on the Baath Party as the primary legitimizer and consequently the main security pillar of the regime.

The situation changed substantially in the late 1970s and early 1980s. The growing opposition of a well-organized and highly fanatical Islamic Front to the regime led to a number of bloody encounters, culminating in the uprising in the conservative Sunni city of Hama in February 1982. During three weeks of utmost brutality, thousands of Muslim fighters and innocent civilians were killed and almost half the city was razed to the ground, primarily by units of Rif'at's Alawi forces. Increasingly, President Assad had to depend on his own community for political survival. More important in public perception, Rif'at and his Alawi forces became far more visible and active in the Syrian body politic in the 1980s. Thus, particularly between the Hama uprising in February 1982 and the Israeli invasion of Lebanon in June 1982, President Assad's regime went through probably its weakest period in terms of mass support. The Sunni majority regarded it as a blatantly sectarian regime, wholly dependent on coercion ruthlessly perpetrated by members of the minority sect.

The regime's projection of its "steadfast" policies in the wake of Israel's invasion of Lebanon was thus an effort to regain the legitimacy it had lost after February 1982. President Assad's vigorous and skillful portrayal of Syria as the heroic defender of Arab rights would, it was no doubt hoped, create an image of his regime as more Arab and less Alawi. Whatever the sectarian affiliations of his regime, President Assad would be embraced by the virulently Arabist Syrian population as a true and committed Arab leader. Assad, known as an avid student of history, must have been impressed by the high status in Near Eastern history of the men who saved the Arab and Islamic world from extinction: Salah al-Din al-Ayyubi, who defeated the Crusaders in 1187, and Baybars al-Bunduqdari, who defeated the Mongols in 1260. What Arab today would consider these men anything but true blue-blooded Arabs? Yet the former was a Kurd and the latter a Turkoman. And while Assad is aware that there is as yet no twentieth-century Salah al-Din or Baybars, he also knows from historical precedent that to fight, or to project himself as fighting, on behalf of the Arab nation could erase from peoples' perceptions the regime's Alawi affiliations.

The stormy relationship between the Syrian regime and the Palestinian leadership in the post-1982 period probably can best be understood within this context. Beyond Syria's ideological commitment to the Palestinian cause, it is the Syrian leaders' need for domestic and Arab legitimization that imposes upon Damascus a highly and visibly activist policy on behalf of one of the most central of Arab concerns: the Palestinian cause.

Syria's efforts and "sacrifices" on behalf of the Palestinians have thus had a price which the Palestinian leaders were to find increasingly unacceptable; namely, the submergence of their interest to that of Syria. The perception of Syria as the primary defender of the Palestinians in the Arab world would bestow on the Assad regime the legitimacy it had always sought, especially after the carnage of Hama. And in jealously guarding this relationship, the Syrians would allow neither the other Arab regimes to act as patrons to the Palestinians, nor the Palestinians themselves to seek the kind of Arab support that might undermine Syria's influence. This is why the Assad regime reacted with such venom when Arafat, with his military infrastructure decimated, decided in 1983 to join with King Hussein of Jordan in exploring a diplomatic option to the Arab-Israeli impasse.

President Qadhafi's adventures in Africa and in the Arab world may also have been largely undertaken to gain legitimacy. His subversion of neighboring countries like Sudan and Tunisia and his military interventions in Chad and Uganda, even when they were less than successful, transformed Libya from a small and inconsequential North African country in the 1960s to a well-known international actor whose identity and leader had become firmly ensconced in the consciousness of people around the globe by the late 1970s. Merely twenty years earlier the Libyans had not been taken seriously even by their neighbors (themselves hardly prestigious international actors). Now their newly acquired reputation, though gained through unsavory methods, meant that they were no longer ignored by their Arab brethren, or contemptuously dismissed as irrelevant by the international community.[8] Publicity—even bad publicity, it seems—was better than none at all, and and Qadhafi took the credit for Libya's international notoriety.

The United States, under the militant presidency of Ronald Reagan, nevertheless, would not budge from a confrontational course with Qadhafi. Soon after coming into office, the Reagan Administration expelled Libya's diplomatic mission with much fanfare, accusing it of threatening the lives of Libyans residing in the United States. Almost simultaneously the United States abandoned its tacit agreement not to challenge Qadhafi's declaration of the 200-mile territorial waters. Although Qadhafi's claim is unrecognized in international law, there was no real strategic imperative for the American decision. Rather, it was simply that the Reagan Administration had chosen to take a firm stand against Qadhafi, a man whose policies, it felt, were aimed primarily at diminishing the global influence of the United States.

Indeed, President Reagan suggested that he would like to see Qadhafi out of power if the latter was not prepared to accommodate American interests.[9] In August 1981 American naval maneuvers in the Gulf of Sidra precipitated an aerial dogfight in which two Libyan aircraft were shot down. Again in March 1986 American maneuvers were this time challenged by Libyan SAM-5 missiles. This apparently was precisely what the American administration had hoped for. Flexing its muscles, the United States navy proceeded triumphantly to demolish the errant missile sites. A month later, accusing Qadhafi of engineering, or at least supporting, a number of terrorist acts against American citizens, the United States ordered its air force to bomb the Libyan capital Tripoli and Benghazi. Military bases and installations were targeted, but these included Qadhafi's own residence. Civilian casualties were bound to be incurred, and these reportedly included two sons and an adopted daughter of Qadhafi himself.

The Reagan administration, pleased by its resolve, felt that it had taught Qadhafi a lesson, proving to him the folly of confronting American power and, in the process, undermining his authority in Libya. Whether this was a correct assessment of Libya's situation is an open question. On the one hand, it could be a gross misreading of Arab radical politics. Notwithstanding the political capital that was bound to be made by Tripoli of the civilian casualties suffered as a result of the bombing raid, it could be argued that what would ultimately matter to Libyans was not their obvious inability to "win" in their confrontation with the United States, but the confrontation itself. That the most powerful nation on earth should choose to confront Libya, that it did so after months of obsessive concern with the intentions and activities of the Libyan leader could be construed by the Libyan population as proof of their world status.

On the other hand, the "bloody nose" inflicted on the Libyan leader by the Reagan administration could have adverse effects on Qadhafi's prestige and political authority. For ultimately, leaders need more than just promises of the "good fight." As I mentioned earlier, they need to be seen as having succeeded in achieving these stability-inducing ideals. One can even argue that the appearance of success is perhaps more legitimizing than merely fighting the good fight. Thus with time, as the extent of Qadhafi's humiliation begins to gradually sink into the Libyan psyche, particularly if this is accompanied by effective economic sanctions, it is possible that he will no longer be hailed as the courageous defender of Arab rights, or as the leader who dared challenge American global power (as his propagandists depicted him), but as a reckless adventurer who brought shame and despair on his country and people.

And, indeed, in Arab contemporary history there have been stark and costly failures when leaders went too far, miscalculated, and lost—when abject defeat was snatched from the jaws of glorious victory. The radical leaders of today cannot allow themselves to forget the June 1967 war. President Nasser's prestige, which reached its apex in the late 1950s, had been undermined in the mid-1960s by an almost continuous economic crisis, itself exacerbated by

Egypt's morale-sapping and financially ruinous military intervention in Yemen. Moreover, as the acclaimed leader of Arab nationalism, his cautious policy toward Israel, which was in stark contrast to his fiery rhetoric, put his credibility into question among many Egyptians as well as Arabs. When in the spring of 1967, tension on the Syrian-Israeli border abruptly increased with Israeli leaders making veiled threats about the Syrian regime and with rumors circulating about an Israeli massing of troops, the chance for Nasser to seize the moment in order to re-establish his prestige was too tempting. Consequently, in May 1967, he decided to ask the United Nations to pull its peace-keeping forces out of Sinai, to assert Egyptian sovereignty over the port of Sharm al-Sheikh, and to close the Straits of Tiran to Israeli shipping. Once the implementation of these decisions achieved his political objective of restoring his regime's credibility, Nasser, who did not particularly want to fight Israel, began to de-escalate the crisis through superpower diplomacy. He obviously hoped that the superpowers, fearful of being drawn into the conflict, would compel Israel to accept the newly created situation, thereby leaving Nasser with a great nationalist victory that would be personally and ideologically satisfying, silence his critics, and erase from their minds Egypt's economic ills and its disastrous intervention in Yemen. And it almost worked, except for the miscalculation that Israel's leaders were just as adept as Nasser himself at the game of risk-taking.

Although Nasser ruled Egypt until his death in 1970, the end of his charisma and of his almost mystical hold on the masses was signaled by defeat in the June 1967 war. "He would stay in power," Fouad Ajami writes, "not as a confident, vibrant hero, but as a tragic figure, a symbol of better days, an indication of the will to resist."[10] The people stayed with Nasser, and indeed they endured the hardships of defeat with him; but his total hold on their emotions and preferences was a thing of the past.

A n:ore recent example of an Arab leader who used foreign policy to broaden his base of mass support—until he overreached himself—is President Saddam Hussein of Iraq. In Hussein's case, however, the initial efforts at legitimization were made through domestic reforms. Utilizing Iraq's immense oil wealth, Hussein embarked in the mid- and late 1970s on massive development and social welfare programs aimed at broadening his own support base in the country. With an eye toward bridging the gap between rich and poor, he vigorously pursued policies that included rapid improvements in housing, education, and medical services, and he enacted legislation on social security, minimum wages and pension rights.

By 1979, foreign policy was beginning to supplant domestic reform as the main vehicle for Hussein's legitimization. Seizing the opportunity left by Egypt's withdrawal from Arab politics because of Camp David, the Iraqi President embarked on diplomatic activity during 1979 and 1980 aimed at establishing Baghdad as the core of Arab political action and himself as the central figure among Arab leaders. In a speech in April 1980, Hussein declared that Iraq had "always had a unique historical position within the Arab nation" and that "the Iraqi army will remain strong to defend the honor of all Arabs fighting foreign forces."[11] Two months earlier, the President in a much-trumpeted proclamation had enunciated his Arab National Charter, which set forth and communicated to other leaders Hussein's ideas on future Arab political action.

Beyond the Arab world, President Hussein lobbied hard to bring the conference of the leaders of the non-aligned world to Baghdad in September 1982, a move that would have given him the opportunity to assume the mantle of leadership. To pave the way, during 1980 the Iraqi leader invited and received more than thirty Third World heads of state and prime ministers. All this activity certainly had the desired effect. By 1980, Hussein had successfully changed his image from that of a ruthless and somewhat anonymous Party-man in the early 1970s to one of a meritorious and substantial popular leader. With his domestic legitimacy seemingly guaranteed, Hussein, armed with the vociferous ideological approval of the Baath Party and cognizant of Syria's steady descent into Lebanon's abyss, set out to make the 1980s the decade in which he would fill the void in Arab charismatic leadership, vacated by Abd al-Nasser after the 1967 defeat. And the young, ambitious Iraqi President might have succeeded had it not been for the old and frail, but ruthlessly committed, Ayatollah Khomeini.

The entry of Iraq's armed forces into Iran in September 1980 was meant to put an end to the hostile role of Khomeini, thereby securing, once and for all, Hussein's legitimacy. Moreover, reports coming from Iran had pictured the political order as utter chaos, with several competing centers of power more interested in fighting each other than in building a viable political structure. The news about the economy was hardly better. Oil production had fallen sharply; there was a foreign currency reserve crisis; food and consumer shortages were rampant. Most crucially, after the collapse of the Shah's army, Iran's fighting capability was thought to be almost negligible; most of Iran's officer corps had fled, been executed, or put into prison; and the equipment, lacking spare parts, was becoming nearly unusable. What is more, the Iranian clergy had succeeded in alienating almost the entire international community. In short, revolutionary Iran of September 1980 was, by all accounts, an easy target for a bold military operation by the Iraqi leader, irritated by Iran's seemingly limitless hostility toward him and his regime.

Once he was convinced that a military operation against Iran would be successful and not costly, Hussein could see the immediate benefits to him in Iraq and in the Arab world generally with the achievement of this "bold" feat. He would go to the Arab summit conference scheduled for Amman two months later as the first Arab leader since independence who had been able to defeat a foreign enemy. And if he could do it in less than the six days it took Israel to defeat Abd al-Nasser, so much the better. Without question he would immediately be raised to a level above that of Arab competitors, such as Assad, King Hussein, King Khalid of Saudi Arabia, etc. How could anyone challenge the status of the dynamic young leader who had inflicted a humiliating and devastating defeat on a major power that threatened the stability of many Arab regimes? In the exuberant days of 1980 when everything seemed to go well for Iraq, Saddam Hussein perhaps could almost hear the late President Nasser declaring the young leader of Iraq the natural heir to the mantle of Arab leadership. With all this, his legitimacy in Iraq, as the leader who had achieved the ultimate in success, would probably be guaranteed for life.

Iraqi aspirations, however, were to shatter against the rock of religious commitment and revolutionary enthusiasm. The hoped-for swift victory never materialized; instead, the conflict has become a war of attrition that has cost Iraq dearly. Economic development has been arrested and reversed; social cohesion has begun to show signs of strain; and as more and more of Iraq's youth sacrifice their lives in this senseless war, the people's morale has sunk deeper into despair. In their mood of discouragement, they could hardly be expected to applaud the leader who has plunged them into this seemingly unending adversity. It is not that Hussein has completely lost support, since he still retains much good will from earlier days. In any case, Iraqis resent Tehran's insistence on the removal of Hussein as the condition for a cease-fire, for people do not, as a rule, take kindly to foreign powers interfering in their domestic affairs. But the halo of merit and success, so necessary for Hussein's legitimacy, has been tarnished by the war, and he is left to try to restore the shine to his blemished credibility.

Arab radical leaders, therefore, need to be careful, even cautious, lest their quest for success through radical action turns out to be a calamitous blunder. Sometimes, as with the June 1967 war, the descent from glory to grief can be bewilderingly abrupt. It is perhaps because of this that, while military force and subversion have continued to be the quintessential radical weapon, radical leaders (some more than others, naturally) have responded to changes in their environment by turning to diplomacy and by adopting moderation in order to enhance their own legitimacy and the status of their country in the Arab and international systems.

The Algerians have perfected this policy of the dual path. Throughout the 1970s and 1980s they have remained faithful in language and deed to the legacy of their revolutionary past: they have been active, even intransigent, members of the so-called anti-Israel "Rejectionist Front"; they have consistently supported the Polisario guerrillas against the pro-Western Moroccan regime, and have called for the establishment of a "progressive," "socialist" republic in the Western Sahara; they have consistently espoused anti-imperialist, and therefore anti-American, causes; and frequently throughout the 1970s they made Algeria a haven for international revolutionary and terrorist groups. On the other hand, the Algerian leaders have been cognizant of the benefits that can accrue to the regime and the country from the pursuit of non-radical policies.

Insisting on the purity of their radical creed, the Algerians have also become masters at diplomatic mediation. They were directly involved in resolving the 1977 border conflict between Libya and Egypt. It was the late President Houari Boumedienne who brought Saddam Hussein of Iraq and the late Shah of Iran together in March 1975 to sign the Algiers Accord, which settled the territorial disputes between the two nations and led to the end of the Kurdish re-

bellion in northern Iraq. In the 1980s the Algerians, more than anyone else, tried valiantly, albeit to no avail, to bring an end to the
senseless slaughter of the Iraq-Iran war. Indeed, Algeria's reputation as a mediating power had become such that it came as no sur-
prise when in 1980 the Algerians were called upon to undertake the
difficult, but eventually successful, negotiations over the American
hostages between Iran's Islamic revolutionaries and the world's
greatest status quo power. Today, throughout the Middle East and
the Third World, Algeria is regarded as a radical and principled
state, yet a pragmatic and rational one. Unquestionably, such a perception cannot but cement the legitimacy of Algeria's leaders and
the regional and international status of their country.

Perhaps with less sophistication than the Algerians, other
Arab radical countries have also responded to changes in the political milieu by adopting more pragmatic policies. Even Libya's Qadhafi, perceived by many Westerners to be pathologically anti-Western, has in fact treated the huge multinational oil companies (the
epitome of Western "capitalist imperialism") operating in his country in a far more cooperative manner than many other Middle Eastern countries that are considered more moderate than Libya. For
example, in contrast to Saudi Arabia, Kuwait, the United Arab
Emirates and Iraq, which had all by 1980–81 completely nationalized their oil industries, Libya up until mid-1986 still allowed a
number of Western oil companies to operate in the country on an
interest-sharing basis.

Qadhafi's relative moderation toward the oil companies was
indicative of his unwillingness to bite the hand that was feeding
him. He, himself, rationalized his dichotomous dependence on the
international capitalist economy by arguing that the oil revenues
were reparations from the industrial world for the damage done to
Libya during the colonial period. In reality, it was the multination-
als' efficiency that provided the necessary revenues for the domestic services (e.g., housing, education, medical care, transportation
system, etc.) on which Libya's high standard of living depended. In
short, Qadhafi's relative moderation and pragmatism in this area
stemmed from an awareness that the uninterrupted flow of oil
money not only financed his radical policies, but also allowed him
to institute domestic social and economic reform and improvements that would cement his image as a meritorious leader.

The avowedly Marxist regime of South Yemen has also endeavored, in certain periods, to moderate its policies for purposes of gaining domestic support. This was particularly the case after the ouster of the hardline ideologue Abd al-Fattah Ismael by Ali Nasser in 1980. Nasser's policies, much more pragmatic than those of his predecessor, seem to have been intended to appease deeply ingrained attitudes of the South Yemen population. Despite all the efforts at Marxist indoctrination, the bulk of South Yemeni society continues to be tribal and conservative, and consequently most South Yemenis regard as alien the regime's radical views and policies on the role of Islam, the family, women, culture and ethics.

Such a conservative society was highly unlikely to endorse the regime's agenda (vigorously pursued by Ismael) of working for the victory of the socialist revolution abroad, particularly as Ismael's revolutionary energy was largely directed, quite naturally, at the countries of the Arabian Peninsula. Tens of thousands of South Yemenis work in the Gulf states, and an aggressive South Yemeni policy toward its wealthier neighbors would alienate not only these numerous Yemeni migrants, but also their extended families who benefit considerably from the remittances of the Yemeni expatriates.[12] Moreover, Saudi Arabia and the other Gulf states themselves continued to offer the carrot of financial aid to South Yemen on condition that Aden temper its destabilizing activities in the area.

Ali Nasser went to considerable lengths to demonstrate to his countrymen his efforts to improve South Yemen's relations with its neighbors. Visits by and to other Arab leaders were well publicized, as was South Yemen's participation in Arab and Islamic forums. Aden's attacks on the Saudi Royal family almost completely ceased, and Nasser began to refer to Saudi kings and princes as brothers, and to Saudi Arabia and South Yemen as the two sister countries.

Likewise, relations with North Yemen improved considerably, particularly after Aden's support for underground opposition to the Sana' government slackened after 1982. Indeed, the presidents of the two countries traveled together on the same plane to Saudi Arabia and elsewhere in the region in 1982. Nasser was no doubt hoping that people would take note of South Yemen's pragmatism. Aden even made overtures to the Sultanate of Muscat and Oman, hitherto regarded as the most reactionary of Arab states. In June

1982 South Yemeni and Omani delegations met for the first time, and a reconciliation agreement was signed. Soon thereafter, Aden's support for the Popular Front for the Liberation of Oman (PFLO) greatly diminished.

South Yemen's moderation was clearly associated with Ali Nasser. Because of its appeal to the rank and file of South Yemeni society, the country's pragmatism in the 1980s was gradually elevating the President to a preponderate position in the party. It was at this point that Nasser should have heeded the danger signs, for the history of the FLN-YSP shows that the party does not relinquish power or abandon orthodoxy easily. Nasser needed to convince the YSP that his moderation and efforts to improve the country's relations with conservative Arab and Islamic states was not meant to erode or slow down the imposition of the Marxist creed on South Yemeni society. He also needed to assure the Soviet Union that his moderation in foreign policy would not weaken Aden's relations with Moscow. Nasser's bloody ouster in January 1986 shows that he was unable to allay the increasing concern of the YSP and its mentor, the Soviet Union.

How close then are Soviet ties with radical Arab regimes, and to what extent has Moscow influenced the foreign policies of the Arab radicals? The Marxist South Yemeni regime naturally has the closest relations with the Communist superpower. It was the Soviet Union which urged on Aden a policy of radical social transformation, and creation of the Yemeni Socialist Party (YSP) as a vanguard Marxist-Leninist party was certainly encouraged, probably even insisted on, by Moscow. After earlier Soviet disappointment with the failure of the socialist experiments in Egypt, Sudan and Somalia, Moscow seems now to believe that a cadre party is the best method to keep Third World allies radical and consistently oriented to the Soviet Union. Apart from access to strategically significant military facilities, the Kremlin benefits from South Yemen's public adherence to Marxism-Leninism, positing the Aden regime as not only a working role model but also an ideological gain for Moscow.

On the other hand, and paradoxically, it is a mistake to think that South Yemeni radicalism in the past has been solely a response to Soviet influence and demands. The Soviets have consistently voiced their interest in establishing diplomatic and economic relations with Saudi Arabia, Oman and the other Gulf states (by 1985, the Soviets had succeeded in establishing relations with Kuwait, Oman and the UAE). Aggressive South Yemeni behavior against these countries would run counter to Soviet intentions, and would almost certainly (as it has in the past) drive them further into U.S. and western arms. Perhaps for this reason Moscow not only did not interfere in Nasser's ouster of the militant Ismael, but also for some time did not stop Nasser from pursuing conciliatory policies toward the conservative regimes of the Arabian Peninsula.

By the same token, Moscow has to ensure that South Yemeni radicalism is not diluted to an extent that would undermine Aden's dependence on the Kremlin. In 1984, for example, a major article in *Pravda* reminded President Ali Nasser's regime of Saudi Arabia's allegedly continuing efforts to subvert South Yemen, thus cautioning it to be careful and less eager in its dealings with the conservative, pro-American kingdom.[13] There are thus clear limits to South Yemeni moderation that Aden cannot transgress. And any leader of South Yemen needs to understand that he may pursue his pragmatist line so long as he does not ignore the client status of his Marxist-Leninist regime.

It has been argued that the Treaty of Friendship and Cooperation signed between the two countries in 1979 is another means by which Moscow maintains its grip on Aden. Maybe so. But similar treaties certainly do not seem to have had that effect on the policies of other radical Arab states such as Syria, which is usually viewed in the West as second only to South Yemen in its political dependence on the Soviet Union.

From 1955 onward, Syria was indeed a firm ally of the Soviet Union, receiving massive military and economic aid. Political, defense and cultural exchanges occurred at every level, and delegations representing a variety of bureaucratic, military and party institutions exchanged frequent visits throughout the 1970s and 1980s. In the words of the Secretary-General of the Baath Party, the understanding between Syria and the Soviet Union was "deep-rooted and bound to develop and expand."[14] Indeed as the regime's internal problems mounted in the late 1970s, it increasingly looked to Moscow for support to safeguard its security, a process culminating in the signing of the Friendship and Cooperation Treaty with the U.S.S.R. in October 1980.

It would be wholly erroneous, however, to think of Syria as

merely a dependent client of the Soviet Union. The past has shown time and again that when its own interest did not coincide with those of Moscow, the Assad regime has acted independently and sometimes in defiance of the express wishes of the Kremlin. For instance, as a result of Syria's military intervention against the leftist-Palestinian alliance in Lebanon in June 1976, President Brezhnev dispatched two strongly worded letters to President Assad, demanding an immediate end to the Syrian operation. Brezhnev was particularly irked because Soviet Prime Minister Kosygin was in Damascus at the time of the Syrian invasion, and only learned of the intervention through his embassy. No apologies, however, were offered by Assad for the Syrian operation. His reply to Brezhnev's letter simply stated that Syria's position was "not subject to compromise because it was based on firm national principles and interest."[15] Syria's obstinate stand persisted even in face of a severance of Soviet military aid and a perceptible deterioration in Soviet-Syrian relations. Friendly relations were not restored until ten months later during Assad's official visit to the U.S.S.R. in April 1977. By then, Syria had achieved all of its stated goals, to which Moscow had so vigorously objected.

Again, in the wake of Israel's June 1982 invasion of Lebanon and the massive aircraft losses Syria suffered, the Syrians demanded immediate Soviet replacement of their losses with more sophisticated planes. The Syrians openly complained that Soviet arms deliveries had been of a vastly inferior nature to the arms supplied to Israel by the United States. In October 1982, Syria's Minister of Information told Western journalists that although Moscow was resupplying planes and equipment lost in the fighting, the quality of Soviet equipment left a lot to be desired.[16] In the wake of these accusations, Damascus downgraded its relations with Moscow. For example, the second anniversary of the signing of the Friendship and Cooperation Treaty went almost unnoticed in Damascus, and the reception organized in Moscow to mark the event was not even attended by the Syrian ambassador, who sent his chargé d'affaires instead. Relations improved only in 1983 after Andropov's assumption of power in Moscow and his decision to supply the Syrians with sophisticated aircraft and missile systems. In all these ups and downs, the treaty had little effect on Syrian attitudes.

Nor was Iraq seemingly bound by its own treaty with the Soviets, which was signed as early as 1972. At that time, and during the first half of the 1970s, Iraq's militant and aggressively radical foreign policy propelled it toward the Soviet Union, and indeed in the same year that the treaty was signed, the Communist Party of Iraq was invited to join the Baath Party in a government of National Unity.

Yet, it was Hussein's decision to move against the Iraqi communists in 1978–79 which precipitated a quick decline in Soviet fortunes in Iraq. In 1978, in addition to widespread arrests, 21 members of the Iraqi Communist Party were executed because of alleged infiltration of the Iraqi armed forces, and another 27 executed in April 1979. Although the Soviets remained publicly silent over the executions, the Iraqis complained that Moscow was withholding military supplies in order to obtain various concessions, including better treatment for the Iraqi communists. The Iraqis were, however, not moved by this Soviet pressure; on the contrary, they decided that henceforth, "Iraq would no longer seek weapons exclusively from the U.S.S.R."[17] By 1982, only two-thirds of its military equipment came from Moscow, as compared to more than 95 percent when the Friendship Treaty was signed in 1972.

Relations cooled considerably so that when the Iraq-Iran war erupted in September 1980, the Soviet Union, although bound by treaty to Baghdad, declared its neutrality and stopped all military shipments to Iraq—an act precipitating intensely hostile public condemnations by the Iraqi leadership. Mirroring the Syrian case, Iraqi-Soviet relations began to improve again only when the Soviets, disappointed by the Iranian revolution and its harsh treatment of members of the pro-Soviet Tudeh Party, decided in late 1982 to resupply Baghdad with weapons embargoed since the outbreak of the war. Iraq's independence was further demonstrated in the post-1982 period, when it consistently upgraded its relations with the United States, leading to the restoration of diplomatic relations between the two countries in 1984.

In terms of military equipment, and thus in a strategic sense, there is probably no Arab regime that is more dependent on the Soviet Union than is Libya. Over 90 percent of its military equipment comes from the U.S.S.R. Between 1976 and 1982, the Libyans paid an estimated $12 billion for Soviet equipment, and about 2,000

Soviet military advisers, and an equal number of East German and Cuban technicians, were estimated to be in Libya.[18] There can be little doubt that Soviet equipment has facilitated a more aggressive and more adventurist Libyan foreign policy.

The primary element of this relationship, however, appears to be commercial, based on Qadhafi's ability to pay for his arms purchases in cash, thus transferring to the Soviet Union badly needed hard currency for its own transactions with the West. For, while Qadhafi's general anti-Western orientation can hardly be objected to by Moscow, his almost obsessive nonconformity makes the Libyan leader difficult to influence, let alone control. Again, while some of his activities, such as his support for Ethiopia, his harassment of Sudan's ex-President Nimeiri, and his support for leftist African regimes (e.g., Ghana, Upper Volta, Guinea, etc.) have served Soviet interests, other policies, particularly his virulent hostility to Mubarak's Egypt, a country with which Moscow has tried very hard to improve relations, could hardly have been welcomed by the Kremlin. Moreover, some of Qadhafi's idiosyncratic antics, such as supporting IRA subversion in the United Kingdom, or exposing his Soviet-trained and equipped armed forces to military defeats in support of Idi Amin, have clearly embarrassed the communist superpower.

Nor could the Soviets forget that in the early 1970s the nationalist Libyan leader declared the Soviet Union to be even more evil than the United States: not only was the Soviet Union equally imperialistic, it was also an atheist power. Those who talk of an ideological affinity between Moscow and Tripoli forget that Qadhafi enthusiastically applauded Sadat's decision to expel the Soviet advisers from Egypt in 1972. Qadhafi is neither ideologically committed nor politically subservient to Moscow, and the Kremlin leaders, who have had their fingers burned many times before by the treacherous fireworks of Arab politics, know that what they have in Libya is a marriage of convenience, which can be severed in the time that it would take Qadhafi to utter three "I divorce thee's."

In Algeria's case, too, whatever influence Moscow has—and that again is negligible—it attained through the sale of military equipment. By the end of the first decade of Algerian statehood, Soviet arms transfers had constituted 90 percent of Algeria's arms purchases. In the second half of the 1970s, Algeria tried to vary its military relations, with half of the arms purchasing agreements signed during that period being with Western countries. Nevertheless, the most expensive and most sophisticated weaponry (such as MIG-25 aircraft, T-72 tanks, and ship-to-ship and ground-to-air missiles) continued to come from the Soviet Union.[19] Between 1976–1981, of the $2.3 billion spent by Algeria on military purchases, $1.8 billion (80 percent) went to Moscow. The pattern does not seem to have changed much in the first half of the 1980s.

But all this arms trade has not been translated by Moscow into political leverage. Whatever the Soviets hoped to achieve, they were bound to fail, given Algeria's almost obsessive commitment to non-alignment. If the notion of non-alignment is a convenient catch-phrase for other Arab and Third World leaders, it represents for the Algerians the only realistic and assertive policy option that the Third World can use to promote a more equitable international order. Consequently, Algeria's non-alignment is not a passive neutrality of the Swiss variety; it is a policy of deciding issues on their merit and in accordance with Algeria's national interest and its ideological worldview. Its policy precludes permanent alignment with, but encourages issue-related support for, one or the other of the superpowers.

Given Algeria's political culture, of which anticolonialism and socialism seem to be prominent features, it is only natural that it finds more in common with the Sovet Union than with the United States. But when Algeria disagreed with the communist superpower, it was quick to show its displeasure. It was thus a signatory to the resolution adopted by the Islamic Conference which "condemned Soviet military aggression against the Afghan people," denouncing it as a "flagrant violation of international law," and calling it "an aggression against human rights and violation of the freedoms of people."[20] Similarly, the Algerians have frequently accused the Soviets of not paying much attention to North-South issues. In short, Algeria is another example of an Arab radical state which may see eye to eye with the Soviet Union on a number of issues, but is in no way subject to Moscow's political dictates.

With the exception of South Yemen, the Arab radical states show no wide-eyed infatuation with the Soviet Union, no desire to regard it as a role-model. Arab radical leaders may share Aden's contention that one could not put the "country's friend and ally, the

Soviet Union, on the same scale with United States imperialism";
one had to make a choice "between good and evil."[21] But on the
whole, the Arab radicals have a much more realistic vision of the
Soviet Union: a friend, yes; but a friend which is a great power with
global interests that include the Arab world and the strategic region
they occupy. In other words, Arab radicals know only too well that
Moscow is in the Middle East for what it can get out of it, and that
inevitably there are bound to be Soviet "transgressions" that will
not be tolerated.

No matter how serious Soviet transgressions are, or may have
been, in radical eyes, they pale into insignificance, however, when
compared with America's. The United States is considered the prin-
cipal threat to progressive regimes. It is seen as aiding the Arab
reactionaries, forever seeking to expand its military presence, demanding hegemonic power in the area, and financing, and sometimes participating in, efforts to subvert radical and progressive
political orders. But most damning of all is the universal perception
that the United States is symbiotically tied to Israel; that without the
massive American military and economic aid, Israel would not have
been able to defeat Arab armies, occupy Arab land, and humiliate
the Arab radicals. On these grounds the Arab radicals, who, apart
from South Yemen, are not ideologically linked to Moscow either in
an intellectual sense or in concrete political terms, draw a distinction between the two superpowers. Qadhafi told a Western jour-
nalist, for example, in 1979: "The Soviet Union is on the side of the
Arabs against Israel. This we consider an anti-imperialist position. .
. . I know that there are two great powers. . . . I also know the
Soviets are our friends."[22] But the most pungent defense of this
position was articulated by President Assad of Syria. Responding to
attacks by Jordan's government that the 1980 Soviet-Syrian Treaty
of Friendship and Cooperation has made Syria into a Soviet satel-
lite, Assad retorted with much relish:

> What harm has the U.S.S.R. done us? Why should we be displeased
> with the U.S.S.R.? The U.S.S.R. supports us in the face of the
> Zionists, who are backed by U.S. arms, ammunition and other means
> of power. Should we reward the U.S.S.R. for all this by putting it on a
> par with the United States, which is giving Israel everything—arms
> and ammunition? Were it not for the United States, Israel would not
> have been able to occupy a single inch of our territory in Palestine or

elsewhere. . . . What does the treaty say? It says that we and the Soviet Union stand, struggle and work against imperialist and racist Zionists. What is there in the treaty that harms the Arabs? Is it in the interests of the Arabs or in the interests of their enemies that the Soviet Union will support Syria and the Arabs in their struggle against racist Zionism? I am not asking any Arab brother to conclude a similar treaty with the Soviet Union. I am saying that I would support any Arab who concludes a similar treaty with the United States, or any Western state, so long that the treaty stipulates that they will side with us against the Zionist invasion. Let King Hussein conclude a treaty with the United States stipulating that America would adopt total neutrality towards the Arab-Israeli conflict. I would relentlessly support and hail such a treaty.[23]

The radical regimes' conduct of their relations with the Soviet Union has been, in a sense, a microcosm of their broader foreign policy behavior in their region and beyond. Two tentative conclusions emerge. First, the radical leaders generally put a high premium on their independence of action and freedom of maneuver to choose the course of action that serves *their* interests (be those ideological or merely self-serving). Second, and because of the above, the level and intensity of their radicalism are usually (admittedly not always) a function of the achievability of the desired goal. If realizing a particular goal necessitates moderate, pragmatic postures, the radical leaders show themselves quite ready to discard revolutionary zeal, at least temporarily. But whatever their course of action, it usually emanates from their perception of the public mood. Ideologically, they cannot risk being too far removed from the people. They also need the halo of merit and success for the purpose of legitimization. And in this, the radical leaders are no different from other leaders in being beholden to the will and whims of their public.

Part Three

The Radical Arab Movements

5

Their Structure
and Beliefs

In Part Two, above, the status quo was defined in terms of the
Arab and Middle Eastern regional order, and any state that
worked to undermine the stability of that order was termed radical. Now, in Chapters 5 and 6, the focus of inquiry shifts to the level
of the Arab state itself. Here, it is the regime, irrespective of its
popularity or perceived legitimacy, that will constitute the status
quo. The analysis in this part, therefore, will concentrate on significant groups and organizations that have been active in undermining the political order of various Arab states. And as I shift attention
from the region as a whole to the micro-level of the state, the reader
should not be surprised to see regimes, such as those of Syria and
Iraq, that have been described as radical on the Middle Eastern regional level, assuming the mantle of the status quo within their own
territorial boundaries as they defend themselves against groups
trying to subvert their political power and authority.

In the 1970s and 1980s, most of the radical groups have tended
to assume a religious identity in the sense that they either have publicly and consciously articulated religious motives and goals, or
have represented religious and sectarian interests. One radical secular movement, however, has been throughout the 1970s and 1980s
a central concern of a number of Arab states, to say nothing of Israel—namely, the Palestine Liberation Organization (PLO). In the

following analysis, I separate the secularist PLO from the religious radical groups, for I can find little that binds the PLO to the various religious movements in terms of history, ideology, organization, or purpose. Consequently, the mode of analysis for this section of the book will be different from the one adopted in analyzing state radicalism. To impose collectivity on the secular and religious Arab radical groups for the purpose of undertaking a thematic analysis is both conceptually artificial and operationally unrealistic. In this and the next chapter, therefore, I shall focus first on the PLO and then examine the religious movements.

The Secular Radical Movements: The Palestine Liberation Organization (PLO)

No cause or issue has so dominated the political and psychological landscape of the Arab world since the end of World War II as has the issue of Palestinian rights. The overlap of Palestinian and Arab nationalisms, and the consequent early and continuing involvement of Arab states in the Palestinian struggle, has tended to make commitment to the Palestinian cause the standard against which Arab regimes, particularly Arab radical regimes, are judged. Moreover, rhetorical support for the Palestinians inevitably pushed the Arab states into military confrontations with Israel that had direct consequences for their separate national interests. Thus in the case of Syria over the Golan Heights, Egypt over Sinai and Jordan over the West Bank, the conflict with Israel in the 1970s was as much a struggle to retrieve land lost to the Jewish state in earlier wars as to ameliorate Palestinian grievances. Because of all these emotional, political, and geo-strategic factors, the PLO, while on many occasions in conflict with various Arab states, has not felt the need to operate *clandestinely* in the Arab world.

The structure of the contemporary PLO is intrinsically linked with the roots of Palestinian nationalism, and the way Palestinian national consciousness developed through the turbulent history of the Arab people in the twentieth century. For, unlike other Third World national movements, Palestinian nationalism grew alongside the more universal Arab nationalism. The relationship between the two has mirrored the wider human and political relationship that has existed between the Palestinian people and the other Arabs: close and fraternal in some instances, at other times tense and antagonistic.

In the early twentieth century, Palestinian nationalism began to stir in the consciousness of the Arab people, who considered themselves the legitimate occupants, and by definition the obvious inheritors, of that region of the Ottoman empire known as Palestine. National awareness was in some measure a response to the first phases of Zionist colonization in Palestine, and since Palestinians tended to believe that there existed a de facto alliance between the Zionists and the post-1908 Ottoman authorities (although in reality, the relationship was never very close), the growth of Palestinian nationalism was closely entwined with the rise and development of Arab nationalism.

The United Nations' decision to partition Palestine in 1947, reached under heavy American pressure, and the consequent first Arab-Israeli War of 1948–49 brought home to the Palestinians the unpleasant realization that the Zionists had at their disposal some powerful international forces, and that to stand any chance of effectively combatting them politically and militarily, Palestinians needed strong Arab backing. With the absorption into Arab countries of thousands of Palestinian refugees in the wake of the 1948–49 Arab-Israeli War, Palestinian nationalism for the next two decades became reliant on, almost subsumed under, Arab nationalism.

Many Palestinians during this period were ardent supporters of the revolutionary policies of Egypt and its radical President Gamal Abd al-Nasser. Believing that the path to Palestine started from, and led through, the Arab capitals, Palestinians also joined other radical Arab parties and groups. They played a role in the Baath, the Syrian Nationalist Party (the PPS), the Jordanian and other Arab Communist Parties, and various Arab nationalist groupings, notably the Arab Nationalist Movement (ANM).

As long as Arab nationalism, led by Abd al-Nasser, and to a lesser extent by the Baath, continued to exhibit the vibrancy and sense of purpose that seemed destined to transform the region, the Palestinians were content to believe that the liberation of Palestine was not simply a Palestinian concern but a wider Arab cause. But when, particularly after the collapse of the Nasser-led United Arab Repub-

lic in 1961 and the ignominious failure of the 1963 unity talks between the radical regimes of Egypt, Iraq and Syria, Arab
nationalism began to show frailties that had gone unnoticed in the
earlier euphoria of revolutionary passion, Palestinians, dazzled by
the example of the Algerian war of independence, began to think in
terms of self-reliance.

By 1965 many Palestinian organizations had sprung up.[1] At
first, almost all of them were numerically small and very loosely organized, and naturally only a very few of them would survive and
grow. Foremost among the hardier groups was the Palestinian Liberation Movement, better known as al-Fateh, formed by a young
Cairo-educated engineer, Yasser Arafat. Another group, destined
to attain international notoriety, was the Popular Front for the Liberation of Palestine (PFLP) under the leadership of two graduates of
the American University of Beirut, George Habbash and Wadi Haddad. Disillusioned by the perceived failures of Arab nationalism,
they and other Palestinian members of the virulently radical Arab
Nationalist Movement (ANM) of the 1950s and 1960s created the
quasi-Marxist PFLP. A few years later, an even more militant offshoot of the PFLP, called the Democratic Front for the Liberation of
Palestine (DFLP), was to appear under the leadership of Naif
Hawatmeh.

Using Marxist terminology, the PFLP and DFLP argued that a
fundamental ideological and political change in the Arab world as a
whole was a prerequisite for the liberation of Palestine. Palestinian
strength, therefore, should be total in its conception and direction,
aimed at the entire region and not limited solely to Israel. Fateh, on
the other hand, affirmed its commitment to direct action against Israel and to noninterference in the affairs of Arab states.

Well aware of the rise of Palestinian militancy, some Arab
states, particularly the radical ones, endeavored to create a Palestinian organization that would represent the aspirations of its people
but would also be institutionalized in the Arab regional system.
Over 400 Palestinians thus attended the First Palestine National
Council (PNC) in May 1964, drew up a national charter, and affirmed the creation of the PLO. In September 1964, at the Summit
Meeting of Arab Heads of State, the PLO was accorded the pan-
Arab stamp of legitimacy.

Dominated by traditional Palestinian notables, the PLO was

not able to attract the younger, more militant generation. Most of the resistance groups declined to join the PLO, preferring to chart for themselves a "revolutionary" course independent of the Arab governments. Nevertheless, while these groups continued to attract new adherents and gather strength, Egypt and the Arab radical states were still the dominant political and military force in the area, and Arab nationalism, admittedly having lost ground from the heady days of the 1950s, was still the most potent ideological force. While the various guerrilla groups were clandestinely acquiring new members, the PLO of the traditionalists and notables continued to receive the patronage of the Arab system and whatever legitimacy that bestowed.

All this changed abruptly and fundamentally after the Arab defeat in the June 1967 Arab-Israeli War. When the Palestine National Council met in July 1968, it was attended for the first time by the various guerrilla organizations; and in the next session, held in February 1969, Yasser Arafat, the leader of al-Fateh, was elected chairman of the PLO. From then on, effective leadership of the Palestinian people resided, seemingly irrevocably, in the hands of the young militants. Also, from that point onward, Palestinian nationalism emerged as a distinct focus of Palestinian devotion, separate from, but linked to, the broader and all-engulfing Arab nationalism. Thus in a recent survey of the Shatilla refugee camp in Beirut,[2] 80 percent of the respondents identified themselves as Palestinian Arabs, whereas only 3.5 percent saw themselves as just Arabs; 88 percent displayed a strong feeling of belonging to Palestine, and 94 percent preferred to marry only fellow Palestinians.

It is not that they reject their Arabness; but, unlike the earlier period, Palestinians in the 1970s and 1980s have come to regard their contemporary situation, as well as their future aspirations, as requiring manifestly Palestinian efforts and sacrifices. On the other hand, they are also aware not only of the Arab bond, but also of the limitations of their own situation. Not only are they a people without a land; they are almost entirely dependent on the good will of the Arab governments for logistical, material and financial support. The history of PLO relations with the Arab states since 1968 (elaborated in the next chapter) is a clear manifestation of the continuous tensions and contradictions inherent in the PLO's definition of its own ideological and political priorities on the one hand, and the constraining imperatives of its objective situation on the other hand.

Decision-Making Elite

For a non-state organization that continues to fragment, the PLO has a very sophisticated network of political institutions. At the very basis of this political structure, the Palestine National Council (PNC) acts as the Palestinian parliament-in-exile and, as such, is the highest policy-making institution of the PLO. Its resolutions are accepted as guidelines to the Executive Committee and form the basis of PLO policies. Because of the dispersal of the Palestinian people, no elections are possible; instead, members of the PNC are nominated by a committee of the preceding council, which ensures the representation of the various strands and groups of the Palestinian movement. Consequently, not only the guerrilla groups are represented, but also trade unions, professional organizations, and independents drawn from around the world. For example, two American academics, Professor Edward Said of Columbia University and Professor Ibrahim Abu-Lughood of Northwestern University, are members of the PNC. In 1983, the following guerrilla groups were represented in the PNC: The Palestine Liberation Movement (Fateh), The Popular Front for the Liberation of Palestine (PFLP), The Democratic Front for the Liberation of Palestine (DFLP), Al-Saiqa, The Arab Liberation Front (ALF), The Popular Front for the Liberation of Palestine, General Command (PFLP-GC), The Palestine Liberation Front (PLF), and the Palestine Popular Struggle Front (PPSF). Ten Palestinian unions and syndicates for workers, intellectuals and professionals were also represented.[3]

Because the PNC meets only once a year (and sometimes due to postponements this period has been longer—e.g., the sixteenth session of the PNC met in February 1983, the seventeenth session did not convene until November 1984), a smaller 14- or 15-member group, elected by the PNC, is entrusted with running the day-to-day business of the PLO. Known as the Executive Committee, this group is the highest executive body in the PLO, commanding full operational authority over all PLO institutions.

While other decision-making institutions, such as the Central

Council and various PLO Departments, participate in policy formulation and implementation, it is the Executive Committee which clearly dominates the decision-making process. And since it is immensely important for the PLO to ensure a semblance of unity (at the very least, unity of purpose) at the highest decision-making level, the members of the Executive Committee have usually come from the various guerrilla groups. For instance, the members of the committee elected by the sixteenth PNC session in February 1983 came from al-Fateh, the PFLP, DFLP, ALF, PLF, PFLP-GC, al-Saiqa, and included some independents.

Because of this diversity of institutional representation, the powers of the chairman of the PLO, Yasser Arafat, are severely restricted. The Executive Committee has seen to it that the personalized character of Arab political culture, so prevalent everywhere and particularly among the Arab radical states, would not take root in this most radical of Arab organizations. Arafat, unlike other Arab leaders, cannot impose his will on Palestinian political institutions; he can persuade, he can demand, he can cajole, but he cannot override the objections of the Executive Committee.

To be sure, Arafat, while by no means a charismatic figure, has nevertheless become for most Palestinians the symbol of their aspirations. Time and again powerful individuals and groups from within and outside the PLO have tried to undermine his authority and legitimacy, but they have consistently failed. With all his political failures, personal weaknesses, and the military humiliations he has suffered, there can be little doubt that the majority of the Palestinian people in the camps, in Gaza and the West Bank, and throughout the Arab world, are behind Arafat's leadership. None of Arafat's competitors and antagonists has his political credibility among the mass of Palestinian people. According to a Palestinian resident of the West Bank, the militant Palestinian leader, Ahmad Jibril, who had been at odds with Arafat for some time, would "not get a job collecting garbage" in his town.[4] Among all Palestinian leaders, Arafat has, by far, the widest support among the Palestinian population.

Even so, as stated earlier, his political authority has been effectively curtailed by the Executive Committee. Let me illustrate. On April 2–4, 1983, Chairman Arafat and King Hussein of Jordan had several sessions of talks in which they sought to arrive at a joint negotiating position vis-à-vis the Israelis that might be acceptable to Washington. On April 4, a Jordanian-PLO joint commission drafted a statement which was approved by the two leaders, whereby King Hussein would lead a negotiating team including Palestinians who would not be PLO members but would have the organization's approval. The next day, however, the PLO Executive Committee categorically rejected the agreement, objecting specifically to the suggestion that the PLO should surrender its right to be the sole representative of the Palestinian people. Although Arafat reportedly encountered much dissent from the Fateh members of the committee, the real opposition came from the members of the other guerrilla groups. On April 8, Arafat sent a message to King Hussein informing him that the Executive Committee was not prepared to give the Jordanian monarch a mandate to negotiate on the PLO's behalf. Not only was Arafat unable to impose his will on the committee, but he apparently was forced to harden his position. On May 15, he asserted in a speech to the PLO officials in Damascus that "the PLO must resume its role of struggle in order to emerge from the current Arab impasse, and effective war from the practical level is now the only available means of recharting the political map."[5]

It is not at all certain that had he not been forced to contend with the militant positions of the other guerrilla groups, Arafat would have been able to persuade the Fateh members and the independents. But the question is academic. Until 1984, Arafat had been particularly sensitive to the notion of Palestinian "consensus," a notion that had tended to give the other much smaller guerrilla groups disproportionate powers of veto. Furthermore, the chairman of the PLO was well aware that the power of these groups hardly stemmed from their ideological purity, military capability, or popular support; it was the power of the various patron Arab states that enabled these groups, numerically small, sometimes even insignificant, to exert so much influence in PLO decision-making. Thus, at various times for example, the ALF and the PLF have been financially and materially supported by Iraq and Syria, al-Saiqa by Syria, the PFLP and the DFLP by Syria, Libya and South Yemen, and the PFLP-GC by Syria and Libya. Needing the support of the radical Arab states, Arafat and al-Fateh gradually became hostages to the will, and more often than not to the whims, of the Palestinian clients of these states.

It was Arafat's break with Damascus during 1983–84 that enabled the Fateh leader to pursue a more flexible PLO policy. The break with Syria divided the Palestinian movement into three factions:

(1) The numerically preponderant Arafat loyalists, most of whom were drawn from the ranks of the Fateh guerrilla organization. A vast majority of the PNC "independents" would consider themselves part of this group. There can be little doubt that this group enjoyed by far the greatest credibility among the Palestinian population as a whole, particularly among the residents of the West Bank and Gaza.

(2) The National Alliance, which was based in Damascus and tended to be an arm of the Syrian government, consisted of Fateh members who rebelled against Arafat because of what they regarded as an increasingly corrupt political leadership. They also disapproved of Arafat's management of Palestinian affairs during Israel's invasion of Lebanon in 1982. Additionally, the pro-Syrian faction of the ALF, PLF, the PFLP-GC and al-Saiqa make up the membership of this group. The National Alliance, consistently echoing the demands of the Syrian government, repeatedly called for the resignation of Arafat, who it labelled "deviationist and capitulationist."

(3) The Democratic Alliance. Composed of PFLP, DFLP, and Palestinian communists, this basically Marxist-Leninist group expressed sympathy for the Fateh rebels. Being less dependent on Damascus, however, it tried during 1984 to engage in a dialogue with the mainstream Fateh members. However, ideological polarity and intense Syrian and Libyan pressure prevented a meaningful rapprochement.

Freed from the constraining influence of other groups, Arafat and the Fateh mainstream leadership called a meeting of the PNC in November 1984, which, significantly, was held in Amman. A new Executive Committee of nine members (five seats were left vacant ostensibly for dissident groups) consisted of Arafat loyalists. The PNC meeting empowered the PLO chairman and the Executive Committee to coordinate efforts with Jordan, and it endorsed

Arafat's earlier visit to Egypt, which had been bitterly condemned by the Palestinian militants and by the radical regimes of Syria and Libya.

No longer imprisoned by the requirements of PLO consensus, and by the resulting veto power of small (in some cases insignificantly small) guerrilla groups, Arafat and the other Fateh leaders embarked upon a peace initiative necessitating crucial compromises that would have been considered unthinkable merely two years earlier. What all this might mean for the Palestinian cause is difficult to assess because disagreement (even within the Fateh leadership itself) with the new orientation continues. The unilateral termination by King Hussein of the year-long joint Jordanian-PLO effort to reach agreement on a Middle East peace in February 1986 shows that when it comes to difficult and significant decisions affecting the future, the well-being, even the very essence, of not only the PLO but also the Palestinian people as a whole, Arafat is still unable to carry his major Fateh lieutenants along with him. What is more, the constellation of forces in the Arab world during the mid-1980s tended to leave Arafat little room for maneuver. Indeed, during this period, there seemed to be more and more Arab states and leaders working with mounting vigor to erode Arafat's authority within the PLO and his influence in the Arab world generally. Hussein's crackdown on PLO activity in Jordan in July 1986, entailing the closing down of PLO offices and the expulsion of key PLO leaders, was a chilling reminder to Arafat and his lieutenants of the perilous shifts in the tides of Arab politics. Even so, what may be indicative of future PLO policy directions is that the Amman 1984 PNC meeting radically changed the intellectual basis of PLO decision-making. The earlier reliance on consensus was abandoned, paving the way for policy-making drawing on majority support.

The Religious Radical Movements

Until the 1970s, especially with the eruption of the Iranian revolution in 1978–79, religious radicalism had little appeal among an Arab population fired by the premises and promises of a pan-Arab secular nationalism. True, the defeat of Arab nationalism in the

June 1967 Arab-Israeli War opened the way for an Islamic resurgence; but for a long period afterwards, it was a form of conservative, "institutionalized" rather than "radical," Islam which dominated the Arab political arena. Only in the latter half of the 1970s did radical, revolutionary Islam truly come into its own.

Because radical Islamic groups lacked a transnational dimension until the late 1970s, generally confining themselves to their own states and operating in their immediate environment, Arab regimes, whether secular or Islamic, had no great need to meet (except in a superficial fashion) the demands of their Islamic opposition groups in the way that they have had constantly to cater to Palestinian aspirations. Islamic groups have thus had to organize and operate mostly in a clandestine fashion.

These origins have naturally precluded the development of complex institutional structures comparable to the ones formed by the PLO. At best, these radical Islamic organizations would boast a "Higher Council" that would consist of a few individuals leading the *jihad* (the holy struggle) operationally and doctrinally. But on the whole, leaderships of the Islamic opposition groups have been highly centralized in the hands of authoritative individuals, acting as charismatic/religious figures and/or para-military commanders. This tendency toward centralization of authority is cemented by the political culture of Islam where, as already explained, political and religious authority has traditionally resided in the person of the leader (al-Khalifa, al-Imam, etc.) rather than in complex and amorphous institutions. It is therefore hardly surprising that historically these movements have tended to flourish under a strong charismatic leadership, and to go into periods of decline and fragmentation in the absence of an identifiable and revered central authority.

Consider the turbulent history of the Muslim Brotherhood in Egypt. Founded in 1928 by Hassan al-Banna, the Muslim Brothers grew in less than two decades into a major grass-roots political organization, claiming perhaps as many as half a million followers. The organization's rapid growth was a classic example of the confluence of political environment and charisma. The 1930s and 1940s were volatile years in Egypt's history. Having gained independence in 1922 from Britain (only partially in the eyes of many nationalists), Egypt was thrust into the usual acute problems of so-

cial, economic and political development, made even more intense
by persistent conflict with the remaining British presence in the
Suez Canal basin. The Brotherhood's establishment and growth
constituted but one response to Egypt's social and political crisis.
Banna's remedy for rectifying the country's ills through a return to a
puritanical form of Islamic observance, including an Islamic government based on the Koran, certainly had much appeal to a basically conservative society. Even so, the Brotherhood's popularity
could not have gained the heights it reached in the 1940s had it not
been for Banna's charismatic leadership. An inspirational leader,
Banna, throughout his life, was the Brotherhood. The organization's ideology, its program for social and political action, were
merely the extension of its leader's energy, personality and vision
for the future.

With Banna's assassination in 1949, the Brotherhood's growth
slowed down considerably. Again, there indeed were objective en-
vironmental reasons for the slump. The Egyptian monarchy had
been replaced in 1952 by the charismatic Abd al-Nasser and his revolutionary brand of Arab nationalism. Not only was Nasser able to
steal the Brotherhood's thunder by providing the Egyptians and
the Arab masses beyond with an attractive and vigorous ideological
alternative, but in 1954, after a foiled assassination attempt on his
life by a Muslim brother, Nasser ruthlessly suppressed the organization, imprisoning some 4,000 members and decimating its leadership.

The Brotherhood could have fared better in the 1950s against
the Nasserist onslaught had it not had a weak and divided leadership. Stripped of its inspirational center, the organization in the second half of the 1950s operated almost half-heartedly at the margins
of revolutionary political activity in Egypt. Only with the
emergence of the learned and charismatic Sayyid Qutb as its undisputed leading figure in the early 1960s did the organization begin to
acquire renewed vigor and vitality. Qutb was fortunate in exercis-
ing his inspirational leadership at a time when the dazzle of Nasser's charisma and the halo of his Arab nationalism were beginning
to fade. In the wake of the collapse in 1961 of the United Arab Republic, the first contemporary union between two Arab states
which had symbolized to so many nationalists the genesis of an as-

sertive future, followed a year later by the ruinous and seemingly endless war in Yemen, Nasser and Arab nationalism, although still forces to be reckoned with, no longer seemed invincible. However, here too, it needed a man of the caliber of Qutb to appreciate the changing environment and to use his charisma to rebuild and remold the morale and the commitment of the Brotherhood.

The regime discovered the extent of Qutb's almost messianic leadership in August 1965 when it unearthed a plot by the Brotherhood to assassinate Nasser and overthrow the regime. Even the authorities themselves were stunned by the depth of the organization's grassroots support, and by the reverence the Muslim Brothers had for Sayyid Qutb. And these were not all poor peasants susceptible to the clever manipulations of religious symbolism: of the thousands arrested, many were lawyers, scientists, doctors, businessmen, university professors, school teachers and students. Sayyid Qutb was deemed so dangerous to the Nasserist political order that, even in the face of numerous appeals for clemency from throughout the Arab and Islamic worlds, the Egyptian authorities decided to execute him.

The demise of Qutb and suppression of the organization was followed, particularly after Sadat's assumption of power, by a gradual co-optation of the Islamicist creed into governmental policy orientations. Lacking a charismatic radical figure in the Qutb mold, the Brotherhood was gradually brought throughout the 1970s into the political process. Under the present leadership it seems that the authorities no longer consider the organization to be a potent radical threat to the survival of the political order; the government of President Mubarak turned a blind eye to the Brotherhood's participation in the 1984 general elections under the umbrella of the New Wafd Party, and the Brotherhood leaders expound fully on the organization's ideas in Egyptian magazines and periodicals.

Some young charismatic leader may be waiting in the wings to take over the leadership and transform the organization yet again into an actively radical opposition. But the years of inactivity and lack of inspirational leadership have brought a process of fragmentation difficult to reverse. Militant young radicals, many of them Qutbiyun (followers of Qutb), decided to leave the Brotherhood in the 1970s and form their own revolutionary Islamic groups. And when analysts and commentators have talked about the Islamic fundamentalist threat to Egypt's stability in the 1970s and 1980s, it is to these smaller groups that they have been referring.

The three most prominent of the groups that operated during the presidency of Anwar al-Sadat were al-Tahrir al-Islami (Islamic Liberation), which was responsible for the attack in 1974 on the Technical Military Academy; al-Takfir wal-Higra (Repentance and Holy Flight), which abducted and killed in 1977 a former Minister of Islamic Affairs; and Tanzim al-Gihad (The Holy War Organization) which assassinated President Sadat in 1981. The first two organizations were led by assertive leaders who were able to elicit from their followers total loyalty to their cause and their leadership.

Tanzim al-Gihad was somewhat different in that there seems to have been no discernible leader to the organization.[6] There was a higher council (Majlis al-Shura), the chairman of which was a respected and learned blind professor, whose main function was to issue *fatwas* (religious pronouncements) in support of the Tanzim's activities. But he was by no means the charismatic leader of the group. Indeed, the moving spirits behind Sadat's assassination and a subsequent attack on police headquarters in Upper Egypt were a civilian ideologue and an officer who acted as chief of military operations. It is likely that had either lived (both were executed in 1982), he would have emerged as the Tanzim's undisputed and authoritative leader.

Be that as it may, what emerges from the foregoing account is the fragmentation of the Muslim Brotherhood, once the charismatic leadership of Sayyid Qutb was lost to the loyal followers. A not too dissimilar process occurred in Iraq with the Da'wa (The Call) Party and in Lebanon with the Amal movement. Like the Brotherhood, both have operated as Islamic opposition groups to the established political orders in their respective countries; but unlike the Sunni Muslims of Egypt's Brotherhood, al-Da'wa and Amal are organizations belonging to the Shiite sect of Islam—the tenets of whose religious beliefs and historical development make its adherents even more susceptible than the Sunni Muslims to centralized authority.

When the prophet Muhammed died in 632 A.D., leaving his followers with no prescriptions for determining the succession, Quraysh, his tribe, met and elected the elderly Abu Bakr as the *Khalifa* (successor). In this action lay the seeds of the first split in the

Muslim community, a sizable minority of which believed that the mantle of leadership should have been bestowed on Ali, the prophet's cousin and son-in-law. The Shia, or followers of Ali, found themselves from then on until the early sixteenth century, when the Safavid dynasty made Shiite Islam the official religion of Persia, in constant opposition to the various established Sunni political orders. In 878, the last descendant of Ali, the Twelfth Imam, disappeared, and Shiites believe that he went into a state of occultation, from which he will reappear in the last days before the day of judgement as the *Mahdi* (the Guided One).

This particular belief makes the Shiites more susceptible to personalized authority. For, while the flock awaits the reappearance of the Mahdi, the religious clergy (Imams) are given much political authority and social power as the Mahdi's representatives and the independent interpreters of Shiite law and scripture. It was thus easy for Ayatollah Khomeini to develop the doctrine of *wilayat al-faqih* (government of jurists) in which he argued that, in the absence of al-Mahdi, government should be entrusted to a supreme religious personage to protect society against corruption and inequity.

From the early 1960s until his execution in 1980, the most respected Shiite cleric in Iraq was Imam Muhammed Baqir al-Sadr. A charismatic leader and prolific writer on political, social and religious matters, al-Sadr was the dominant political and religious personality within the Shiite community of Iraq. Whether it was he or someone else who established al-Da'wa (for the party's origins remain unclear), there can be little doubt that during the 1970s, it was al-Sadr who was its inspirational leader.

Operating clandestinely throughout the 1970s, al-Da'wa, aided by Sadr's vigorous and activist leadership of the Shiite community, attracted many followers not only from the poor Shiites of the holy cities of Najaf and Karbala and the Baghdad ghetto areas of al-Thawra and al-Salam, but also many middle class professionals and small businessmen. The rapid growth of the party was spurred immeasurably by the Iranian revolution, which thrust Shiite clergy into power, thus transforming what until then had been a theoretical and intellectual notion into a living reality. The growing number of party members could hope—realistically they thought—to make Baqir al-Sadr, to whom they gave unquestioned allegiance, the Khomeini of Iraq. Unfortunately for al-Sadr and his loyal followers,

President Saddam Hussein and the Baath Party of Iraq shared that view. After some acts of sabotage, al-Sadr was arrested in 1979, then executed in 1980. A similar fate befell more than 500 of his supporters.

After 1980, al-Da'wa went into sharp decline. Part of the reason was the government's ruthless suppression of the party. Another reason was the government's intelligent socio-economic policies, from which the Iraqi Shiite population derived immense benefits, undermining al-Da'wa's support base. But it was the loss of Sadr that did untold harm to al-Da'wa and Shiite oppositional activism generally. No other clergymen could duplicate Sadr's charismatic inspiration, even those suggested by Ayatollah Khomeini from across the border. Consequently, party members, deprived of inspirational leadership, found it increasingly difficulty to stand up to mounting government persecution. At this point, the familiar cycle of fragmentation began to afflict the hitherto united and vigorous al-Da'wa.

By the mid-1980s, Shiite organized opposition in Iraq had split into a number of competing, often conflicting, groups.[7] One group that extricated itself from al-Da'wa in 1980 is Munadhamat al-Amal al-Islami (The Organization for Islamic Action), which opposes the "adventurism" of al-Da'wa. Led by two clerics, Muhammed al-Shirazi and Hadi al-Mudarissi, this group considers long-range planning as the most potent form of combating the government. Antagonistic to and in direct competition with Islamic Action is al-Mujahidin (The Warriors for Islam), who apparently are scornful of clerical political leadership. Meanwhile al-Da'wa itself seems to have split into two conflicting trends, one a reformist group advocating moderation under Sheikh Mahdi al-Khalisi, and the other a militant fundamentalist group loyally supporting Khomeini and led by Hojatilislam Muhammed Baqir al-Hakim. The latter has the personal backing of the Iranian clergy and is Chairman of the Iranian-based Higher Council of the Islamic Revolution, which consists of a number of Iraqi Shiite divines and laymen and is supposedly responsible for directing the Shiite struggle in Iraq. While some acts of sabotage continue in Baghdad, partly due to the decreased internal vigilance of a government concerned mainly with its debilitating war with Iran, there are no signs that the Shiite opposition movement in Iraq has found a charismatic and authoritative figure to lead, unify, and envigorate it.

The story of Shiite opposition to the political and social order in Lebanon, dominated as it was for decades by Maronite Christians and Sunni Muslims, is not dissimilar from the Iraqi Shiite experience. It required a charismatic cleric to deliver the Lebanese Shiites from their political and social inferiority; the charismatic leader then departed the scene, leaving his flock bewildered and resentful, and the movement began to fragment. But there was one crucial difference: the Lebanese Shiites did not have to face a strong, highly centralized, and effectively organized government such as the Baghdad Baathist government. Weakened as they were by the loss of charismatic leadership, the Lebanese Shiites could still mount successful attacks against a collapsing center; and success breeds confidence not only in one's cause, but also in the wisdom and able stewardship of one's leaders.

The historically quiescent Shiite population of Southern Lebanon was galvanized into vigorous political action by the Iranian-born Imam Musa al-Sadr. True, in the late 1950s and 1960s, rapid socio-economic changes were overtaking the nearly forgotten, down-trodden Shiite masses of the South. During this period, large numbers of Shiite youth began to attend newly constructed local schools, and then went to Beirut to attend the new national University of Beirut. Many of the students and other Shiite migrants searching for opportunities in the metropolis lived in the poor suburbs of southern Beirut. Thus, while their own socio-economic status rose considerably and quickly, it was very plain to the Shiites that they remained inferior to the other Lebanese sects. Politicized by their objective conditions, they were indeed ripe for vigorous political activism. But it needed a man of the charisma of Musa al-Sadr to harness, lead and direct this incipient revolutionary energy.

A physically dominating man of high intelligence, personal charm and ceaseless energy, al-Sadr attracted a support base that ranged from the affluent Shiite merchants based in West Africa to Beirut students and the poor, semi-literate peasants residing in Jabal Amil. He quickly filled a leadership vacuum that had arisen from the increasing inability of the traditional Zuama (feudal leaders) to meet the rising political and social expectations of the Shiite

community. In 1968 he forced the Lebanese government to establish the Higher Shiite Islamic Council (HSIC), and a year later he became its president, dealing a formidable blow to the traditional
Zuama. Perhaps his greatest legacy was that, despite deep
sociological differences between the Shiite populations of Beirut,
Jabal Amil and the Beqa Valley, al-Sadr was able in a relatively short
time to give most Shiites an inclusive communal identity, and
simultaneously to change the Lebanese Shiite outlook from one of
submission to one of rebellion and radicalism.[8]

Capitalizing on Shiite unity, al-Sadr organized in the Beqa Valley the largest rally the Lebanese had ever witnessed, during which
he established a grassroots movement which he called Harakat al-
Mahrumeen (The Movement of the Deprived). From this, he
created a para-military arm, Afwaj al-Muqawama al-Lubnaniya
(Battalions of the Lebanese Resistance), which became known by its
acronym, Amal, meaning "hope." By 1978, through the systematic
work of the HSIC and Amal, the Shiite community had developed
an extensive political, social and military infrastructure.

But then, like his namesake in Iraq, the charismatic leader of
Lebanon's Shiites was to depart the scene at a crucial time in his
community's struggle for recognition and power. In August 1978
he traveled to Libya, where he "disappeared." When he was alive,
Imam Musa al-Sadr's charisma could hold the disparate Shiite community together, but no successor had the same kind of inspirational leadership to step into al-Sadr's shoes and be proclaimed undisputed leader of the Shiites. Within the Shiite mainstream political activity, leadership devolved onto three men: Nabih Berri, who
became leader of Amal; Hussein al-Husseini, who, having led Amal
for a year after al-Sadr's disappearance, was elected to the traditionally Shiite position of Speaker of the Lebanese Parliament in 1984;
and Sheikh Muhammed Mahdi Shams al-Din, who took over the
running of HSIC. In the struggle to determine who would represent
the Shiite community, the latter two aligned themselves against
Berri, but the real contest seems to lie between the layman Berri and
the cleric Shams al-Din. The former commands manpower, armed
might, and street support; the latter possesses the symbols of religious esteem and legitimacy. Both, however, belong to the moderate wing of the movement and are willing to achieve their goals by
dealing with the established order.

The militants, who had accepted al-Sadr's leadership (and Sadr was a pragmatist par excellence), were no longer willing to abide by the moderate strictures of the post-Sadr leadership. Hussein Musawi, a militant member of Amal's Command Council, led a revolt against Berri in the summer of 1982. He established himself in the Beqa Valley and, seemingly with Syrian support, created a shadowy organization referred to sometimes as Islamic Jihad, sometimes as Islamic Amal, from a small band of disaffected ex-Amal fighters and some 1,000 Iranian volunteers. This group was implicated in the truck bombings of the United States Embassy and the marine compound in Beirut.

Simultaneously, another militant group, drawing its support primarily from the slum dwellers of southern Beirut, began to assert itself in the capital and beyond. The Hizbollah (The Party of God) recruited followers quickly and in no small numbers. And it was the appealing and lucid Sayyid Muhammed Hussein Fadlallah who proved to be an important recruitment asset for the party.

Along with more than a dozen other splinter groups, Islamic Jihad and Hizbollah mounted concerted terrorist attacks against Israelis, Americans, French and Maronites. By the end of 1983, these groups were threatening to wrest the mantle of Shiite legitimacy from Berri and Amal, for, while he argued, bargained and pleaded, they acted, and acted decisively, ruthlessly and dramatically. Berri had to act; he had to prove once and for all that his group was still the major Shiite fighting force and that he was its leader and authoritative commander. In February 1984 Berri called on Shiite army soldiers to desert the Lebanese army, and then, with the help of the Druze militia, Amal took over control of West Beirut. The following months saw increasing Amal involvement in the fight against the Israeli occupiers of Shiite ancestral land, and then in 1985 Amal took on the PLO in an effort to prevent a return to the pre-June 1982 Palestinian dominance in southern Lebanon.

The loss of Musa al-Sadr was indeed a great blow to the Shiites in Lebanon, but they seem to have survived the loss much better than the Iraqis did when Imam Baqir al-Sadr was executed in 1980. The weakness of the center in Lebanon was the decisive factor. Unlike the pervasive and overpowering presence of the Baath in Iraq, the established Maronite/Sunni order in Lebanon had by 1979 all but collapsed; and Musa al-Sadr's inheritors, lesser men indeed, were still able to partake successfully in the struggle for power. Thus, even with the present absence of charismatic leadership, the Lebanese Shiites' effort to turn the status quo in their favor seems certain to continue primarily, but not exclusively, through Berri's mainstream Amal movement.

I have so far highlighted the seeming indispensability of centralized, inspirational leadership to the health, growth and vigor of Islamic opposition groups. There is, however, an exception to this rule. In their struggle against the Baathist/Alawi regime of Hafiz al-Assad in Syria throughout the 1970s and early 1980s, the Syrian Islamicists have not had a dominating, charismatic figure to lead and inspire them. They have been led by a number of clerical and lay individuals, whose support has on the whole tended to be regionally based. The various leaders, thus, have drawn their followers mainly, but of course by no means exclusively, from the city or region in which they lived and operated.[9]

In October 1980 these various groups and leaders formed themselves into the Syrian Islamic Front. The main force behind its formation and radical activities was Adnan Saad al-Din, and indeed it was the period spanning its birth and its bloody slaughter in Hama in February 1982 that witnessed the Muslim Brotherhood's most intensive activism. Yet, strong-willed and ruthlessly committed as he certainly was, Saad al-Din was no charismatic figure, and the Front remained basically a decentralized organization with an executive committee that neither led nor inspired, but simply coordinated objectives and activities. Indeed, after the bloody defeat of Hama in February 1982, the Front, lacking a charismatic figure and faced with a ruthless and powerful political order, collapsed almost immediately.

The blow that the Syrian government dealt the Muslim Brothers in Syria was so severe that perhaps now only a truly charismatic leader could revitalize the organization. As the historical development of Islamic opposition groups in Egypt, Iraq and Lebanon seems to suggest, charisma and inspirational leadership have tended to hold these groups together in the face of great, sometimes overwhelming odds. Faith, belief and a sense of purpose are powerful motivating tools, but their power is hugely enhanced when they are articulated, even cleverly manipulated, by someone possessing an unusual hold over his people. This does not mean that the groups inevitably cease to function once the leader departs the scene. But charisma adds immeasurably to commitment, and in the face of a formidable foe it is almost a necessity.

Beliefs

At the base of all the Islamic opposition movements lies a fundamental belief in the necessity of imposing Islamic laws and prescriptions on the running of the Muslim states. Within the parameters of this general ideological orientation, however, there exists a wide array of opinion as to the best means of achieving this goal, given the objective conditions in which the various groups have operated. Opinions range from the so-called moderate and pragmatic, advocating, through working within the system, the gradual introduction of Islamic norms of behavior in accordance with the system's capacity to absorb these changes (e.g., Lebanon is obviously a different case from Egypt), to the militant position prescribing, through armed struggle, no less than a complete theocratic state. It is not surprising that the larger, more institutionalized groups tend to exhibit moderate orientations, while the dissident fringe groups inevitably cling to militant positions.

The Sunni organizations of the Muslim Brotherhood in Egypt and in Syria have recently shied away from advocating the establishment of a theocratic state in their respective countries. As Egypt's Brotherhood emerged from the underground to a semi-public position, its radicalism subsided. Banna and Qutb had advocated the transformation of the secular state into an Islamic country through armed *jihad*. But the present leadership under Umar al-Tilmisani has watered down the earlier maximalist position considerably by seemingly deciding to coexist with the secular state (they participated in the 1984 general elections, fielding candidates under the guise of the New Wafd Party), and to work for the gradual infusion of Islamic precepts into the political system.

Similarly, and somewhat surprisingly given its militant history, the Islamic opposition movement in Syria has advocated a relatively moderate ideological position. The charter of the Islamic Front published in 1981 certainly advocates a long-term commit-

ment to the creation of an Islamic state, but it also calls for "separation of powers and the rule of law resting on *shura* [consultation],
guaranteeing individual dignity, freedom, and liberty." Likewise in
a somewhat un-Islamic tone, the charter demands the "strengthening of Arab nationalism and unity in the larger context of Islamic
solidarity."[10] This language is indeed surprising coming from a fundamentalist Islamic group, for, according to Islamic precepts, it is
the broader Islamic *umma* (community), not the ethnic groups
within it, which should be the primary concern of Muslims.

What we see here is a movement that genuinely believes in its
mission, but has had to respond in a pragmatic manner to the objective reality of its situation. Unlike Egypt's Sunni society (90 percent
of Egypt's population is Sunni), Syria has sizable and influential
minorities, foremost among which is the Alawi community, representing approximately 12 percent of the population, from which the
President and some of the key members of the regime are drawn.
Thus the advocacy of a Sunni theocratic state would be less wel-
come in a religiously divided country like Syria than it would be in
Egypt.

The reference to Arab nationalism was also motivated by pragmatic considerations. Representing the clarion call of a Sunni urban
culture, Arab nationalism was an appropriate symbol to remind the
majority Sunni population of Syria of the divide that allegedly sepa-
rates them and their concerns from the ruling Alawi minority. More
important, however, was the Islamic Front's obvious awareness of
Syria's almost obsessive commitment to the concept of Arab
nationalism. As shown in Chapter 3, the Syrians frequently refer to
their country as "the beating heart of Arabism" and have always
considered themselves the most ardent defenders of Arab
nationalist causes. This perception is so powerful that it is shared by
many Arabs outside Syria. Realizing the psychological power of the
concept in Syria, the Muslim activists could not but allude to Arab
nationalism even if in a most fundamental and doctrinal sense Arab
nationalism must be antithetical to the notion of a multi-ethnic,
multi-state Islamic *umma*.

The regime's suppression of the Islamic Front in Hama in February 1982 was so total that there have been few reports of Islamic
opposition since then. It is thus difficult to ascertain the nature of
the ideological split (if indeed there is any) between the mainstream

Brotherhood and some of its smaller, more militant allies. In Egypt, on the other hand, dissident groups challenged Tilmisani's Brotherhood not only through more militant activity, but also through more rigid interpretation of the mission of the Islamic opposition groups. Al-Tahrir al-Islami, al-Takfir wal-Higra, and Tanzim al-Gihad all believed in the forcible imposition of a righteous Muslim state. Working within the system was utterly abhorrent to these groups. Indeed al-Takfir advocated the principle of spiritual separation of the members of the group from the sinful Egyptian society; and in the latter, al-Takfir included the leaders and members of the mainstream Brotherhood. Al-Gihad is even more militant doctrinally. Not only does it seem to use the word infidel liberally by attaching it to almost everybody, but it also considers the resort to violence against infidels an Islamic obligation—the only way. In the trial of the Gihad members who assassinated President Sadat in October 1981, the accused, crammed into large iron-bar cages, persistently threatened Sadat's successor, President Mubarak, that he too would meet the fate of his predecessor. Their leader announced: "We are charged with trying to overthrow the ruling system and establishing an Islamic state. This is an honor for us."[11] These were men who did not fear death, who were messianically committed to the violent overthrow of the existing political order which included, in their eyes, their mother organization, the Muslim Brotherhood.

In the domain of the Shiite oppositional activity, the political thought of Iraq's al-Sadr was far more militant than that of his namesake in Lebanon. Baqir al-Sadr's prescriptions on the nature of the Islamic state have intellectually underpinned much of Khomeini's political activities. Indeed, he is considered by his followers and enemies alike as not just a supporter but an initiator of the Islamic order in Khomeini's Iran. It is argued that he was planning to put his theoretical explications into operation in Iraq as well as in Iran—a belief that led to his execution by the Iraqi authorities in 1980.

It is, however, still unclear whether this indeed was the case. There is no doubt that Sadr's ideological views on the necessity of an Islamic state and on the supreme political role of the *marja* (highest religious authority) would be considered treasonable by the Iraqi regime. However, Sadr's theoretical formulations seemed to relate to an 'ideal type' situation, which could be attainable in Iran where the vast majority of the population is homogeneously Shiite. In Iraq, the Shiites are barely a majority. Over 40 percent of the population is Sunni, highly entrenched in the army, security apparatus, business and the educational institutions.

Not given to self-delusion, Baqir al-Sadr could not have thought that the imposition of his basically Shiite political philosophy on a diverse society such as Iraq, containing a numerous and powerful Sunni community, would stand the slightest chance of success. Rationally, therefore, one would have thought that his vigorous opposition was a manifestation of what he perceived to be, rightly or wrongly, a regime implacably hostile to the political and social interests of the Shiites and utterly dismissive of their religious sensitivities. On the other hand, he, like so many others, may have been swept by the euphoria of Khomeini's success in early 1979 into forgetting, or just belittling, the objective constraints in Iraq's situation.

Musa al-Sadr, the leader of the Shiite Amal movement in Lebanon, as well as his successors in the organization's leadership, seemed to take very much into consideration the objective reality of Lebanon's sectarian system, in which the Shiites form no more than 35 percent of the total population. From the movement's inception, Musa al-Sadr endeavored to allay the fears of the other Lebanese sects by insisting that, while Amal's *raison d'être* emanates from the Shiite historical culture, the organization was meant to represent all of Lebanon's *mahrumeen* (deprived). This concern was enshrined in Amal's charter, drawn up in 1975, which called for the complete abolition of the confessional system in Lebanon and equal rights for all citizens without distinction. Significantly, a number of Christian intellectuals participated in the formulation of the Charter.[12] None of al-Sadr's successors—Berri, Husseini or Shams al-Din—has departed from Amal's original ideology.

Almost inevitably the smaller secessionist groups that broke with Amal after al-Sadr's disappearance took a more militant line. Hussein Musawi's Islamic Jihad, following the dictates of its masters in Tehran, advocates the transformation of Lebanon into a fundamentalist Islamic republic along the line of the present political order in Iran. Musawi's organization may be able to muster the odd suicidal truck, but within Shiite and Lebanese politics as a whole, it is morally and numerically unimportant.

A more significant figure among the fringe Shiite groups is Sayyid Muhammed Fadlallah of Hizbollah, who has attracted a wide following among the Shiite youth in Beirut. Fadlallah's ideas are still unclear. For example, he has called for the eventual establishment of an Islamic state in Lebanon, even though the country has a sizable Christian population. His argument is that, unlike his Christian counterpart, the Muslim is required by the tenets of his faith to live in an Islamic faith: "When a Muslim lives in a state that does not adopt Islam, his life remains confused because of the dualism [of authority] that he is living under. . . . The Christian, by contrast, does not have this problem when living in an Islamic state."[13] In another instance, however, Fadlallah dismisses the idea of an Islamic state, for the "objective conditions are not there for Islam to rule Lebanon."[14]

All the Islamic opposition groups, whether Sunni or Shiite, pragmatic or militant, have had a common ideological thread that has bound them together: their adherence to the tenets of their faith. By definition, therefore, they have all been committed to the ultimate objective of establishing Islamic political orders and to the struggle against "infidel secularists" and their outside supporters. But apart from the fanatical few, these groups have been sensitive to the wide array of objective constraints on the achievement of this goal, and thus most have regarded the creation of a truly Islamic state through militant *jihad* a very long-term goal—even a utopia.

This seeming inability of the various Islamic groups and organizations to achieve the ultimate goal, compounded by the dispiriting resilience of the contemporary Arab state, may explain the discernible decrease in organized Islamic revolutionary activity in the Arab world in the mid-1980s. But even if Islam as a revolution shows signs of being on the decline, this in no way means that the potential for revolution in Arab countries has all but disappeared. The underlying social and economic factors which contributed to the perceptible rise in the intensity of Islamic radicalism during the second half of the 1970s and early 1980s were not eradicated in subsequent years. These radicalizing impulses had been exacerbated by the oil boom of the early 1970s, which had led to an increased level of economic activity not only in the oil-producing countries but generally throughout the Arab world. And as is usually the case, the acceleration of economic activity occurred primarily in the cities and heavy urban areas. Two potentially explosive consequences tended to follow. One was an increasing rural-urban migration and the other a widening socio-economic, and consequently political, gap between rich and poor.

It was, therefore, no coincidence that the main agents of violent dissent in the 1970s and early 1980s were on the one hand traditional peasants and village dwellers who had migrated in increasing numbers to the big cities, and on the other hand, students and an assortment of professionals who had become disillusioned with the corruption, mismanagement, and inequity of political and economic systems. Alienated from the social milieu and the political order and disgusted by the conspicuous consumerism and the lax living of the rich city "effendis,"[15] members of both socio-economic groups were ripe for revolutionary picking.

When it came to choosing a revolutionary path, the socially and economically disinherited, the politically excluded, those on the margins of society in the 1970s, the supposed decade of the plenty, tended to embrace Islamic radical ideology. There were hardly any credible alternatives: revolutionary pan-Arab nationalism had been humiliated in 1967; Marxism and other such globalist ideologies were too esoteric and too divorced from people's own realities; and the modernizing military had by the 1970s clearly failed to deliver on their earlier promise of moral regeneration and social equality. In addition to eternal happiness in the afterlife, the Islamicists, by emphasizing the centrality of justice in Islam,[16] would offer people the promise of social, economic and political justice. And the people, imbued with Islamic values, would readily believe.

The militant Islamic tide reached its peak in the wake of the Islamic revolution in Iran, and many believed during that period that there was no stopping the Islamic march. But the targets of Islam's anger in the Arab world were able to survive. Indeed, compared with the period 1979–82, when militant Islam constituted a most potent challenge to the authority and legitimacy of the state in the Arab world, very little discernible revolutionary activity of any consequence was mounted by the radical Muslim groups after 1982. It may be that, for a number of reasons which I discuss in the conclud-ing chapter, the Islamic euphoria gradually subsided. But Arab governments and leaders can only relax at their peril. So long as cor-ruption, inequities and mismanagement pervade the political and social order, and so long as people believe themselves to be excluded from the body politic, having little or no influence on its direction or say in its reform, radical groups in the Arab world, Is-lamic or non-Islamic, will continue to find a fertile ground for their revolutionary impulses.

6
. . . And Their Crusades

The 1970s was a decade of politically entrenched Arab regimes. Through a combination of a more sophisticated utilization of legitimacy symbols and state institutions on the one hand, and the ruthless use of regime coercion on the other hand, the almost monotonous occurrence of military coups and abrupt and violent changes of government that had characterized the preceding two decades all but disappeared with the onset of the 1970s. Paradoxically, however, the increasing regime stability was accompanied by mounting activism by the PLO and the various radical religious groups. The growing militancy of opposition groups, countered by a more determined state power, meant that the 1970s and 1980s, while relatively stable in terms of regime survival, were perhaps bloodier and more conflict-ridden than the 1950s and 1960s.

PLO Radicalism

In the light of the Palestinians' declared "ideological goal" (al-hadaf al-aqaidi) of constant resistance to the "Zionist state," it is hardly surprising that the development of PLO strategies and politico/

military actions should be intimately and intricately intertwined with the domestic political and foreign policies of Jordan, Lebanon and Syria, the three states contiguous to Israel. In addition to geographic proximity, each of these three states was in its own way an attractive venue for Palestinian political and military activity. Jordan was attractive demographically because the majority of the population, even after the loss of the Palestinian West Bank to Israel in June 1967, was of Palestinian stock. The conflict between the Palestinian guerrillas and the established political order in Jordan in 1967–70 was, in a sense, a struggle for the loyalty of Jordan's Palestinian population. Lebanon's attraction was, basically and cynically, the country's weakness. Torn by sectarian divisions, lacking a strong political center, Lebanon could neither stem the growth of the Palestinian presence, nor check the PLO's mounting activism against Israel and inside Lebanon. Syria's attraction to the Palestinians, on the other hand, was hardly its weakness, for it had a powerful army and strong and ruthless political leadership. It was Syria's radical ideology, based on Baathist nationalist principles, that drew the Palestinians and Syrians together. The relationship would have its ups and downs in the 1970s and 1980s, but for long periods the Palestinians regarded Syria as their natural ally and patron. Later, the Palestinians and the Syrians would become involved, sometimes cooperatively and at other times antagonistically, in the Lebanese civil war, which ultimately cut the PLO down to size. But it was in Jordan in 1970–71 that Palestinian radicalism met its first major setback.

As we have seen, a coherent Palestinian movement began to emerge in 1964 when the second Arab summit conference in Alexandria decided to establish the PLO. But the institutionalized and traditionalist character of the organization, and the fact that it had been created by Arab governments, alienated many of the young Palestinians from the infant organization. This new, highly politicized generation of Palestinians, many of whom had grown up in refugee camps, had begun to despair of the Arab states' ability or willingness to liberate their land for them. As a result, they advocated self-reliance and direct Palestinian action through guerrilla activity; and a number of paramilitary organizations began to operate parallel to, but not necessarily in conflict with, the PLO. The most important of these new groups was al-Fateh, led by Yasser Arafat.

The defeat of the Arab states in the June 1967 Arab-Israeli War increased the prestige of the guerrillas in the Arab world by reinforcing their claim that they alone were capable of realizing Palestinian aspirations. However, the seminal event in the development of the guerrilla movement as a major political force in the Arab world occurred in March 1968 at Karameh in East Jordan, where Palestinian commandos inflicted heavy losses on a large Israeli force sent to destroy guerrilla bases in the town. In military terms, the Israeli operation was successful in that it achieved its basic objective of destroying the guerrilla base. But the heavy casualties the commandos inflicted on the hitherto "invincible" Israelis was hailed by the Arab public as a great victory. The "battle of Karameh" (Karameh meaning "dignity" in Arabic) now became rooted in Palestinian folklore and was the catalyst for the movement's rapid growth.

The dramatic growth in numbers and increasing prestige of the guerrillas were bound to have major repercussions on the domestic situation of those Arab states, particularly Jordan, within whose borders the guerrillas operated. Through an elaborate network of military, social, economic and administrative institutions, the guerrilla camps in Jordan became a state within a state. By the end of 1968 two largely independent political forces existed in Jordan: the Hashemite monarchy and the Palestinian commandos. King Hussein's resentment of this state of affairs and his efforts to confine the power and activity of the guerrillas led to mounting domestic tension. As the year drew to a close the domestic political situation became distinctly polarized between the two major, clearly antagonistic, forces.

In their struggle both Hussein and Arafat sought the support of Egypt's Nasser. While sympathizing with Hussein's protestations against the anarchic activities of the guerrillas inside Jordan, Nasser nevertheless declared himself "fully committed to offering all help to the Palestinian guerrilla action, [since] the emergence of the Palestinian struggle constituted a big transformation of the Arab situation."[1] At the same time, he tried to convince Arafat that the guerrillas would be committing a costly mistake if they thought they were capable of defeating Israel on their own. The nub of this argument was prophetically elucidated by Nasser's confidant, Muhammed Heikal, who maintained that guerrilla action could not be decisive in Palestine where the terrain was open, where the "oppressors" outnumbered the "oppressed," and where, in contrast to Vietnam or Algeria, the guerrillas could not seek immunity from enemy action in friendly territory because Israel possessed the capability of striking anywhere in the Arab world. Thus, the idea that defeating Israel could be achieved through guerrilla action alone was no more than a myth propagated by ill-informed romantics. The task of defeating Israel, Heikal concluded, could only be accomplished by the entire forces of the Arab world, of which the Palestinian resistance was an integral and important part.[2] In trying to convince Arafat of the validity of this argument, the Egyptian leadership hastened to impress upon the guerrilla leader the need for peaceful coexistence inside Jordan so that the capabilities of the Arab forces could be preserved and utilized against the common enemy rather than being expended in internecine fighting.

Had Arafat and his chief lieutenants accepted Egypt's advice and reasoning, they might have saved themselves immense humiliation, and their people much suffering. But they did not. Riding on a tidal wave of Arab euphoria and public support, the Palestinian leaders continued their operations against Israel and increased their domestic challenge to the authority of the Jordanian monarch. By 1970 the collapse of Jordan's fragile domestic structure had become a distinct possibility. In early September, clashes between the Jordanian army and the Palestinian guerrillas mounted in frequency and intensity. Later, after a multiple hijacking operation by the Palestinians, the skirmishes between the guerrillas and the army developed into a bloody, full-scale civil war.

When it was finished eleven days later, the civil war had resulted in the death of some 3,000 Palestinian guerrillas and civilians and the expulsion of the bulk of the Palestinian movement from Jordan. By the end of 1971, when the Jordanian army had ruthlessly eliminated the few remaining PLO positions in northwest Jordan, the sophisticated and complex institutional structure, the state-within-a-state, that the Palestinian leaders had proudly built, was utterly decimated by an Arab army. The Palestinians' first excursion into Arab radical politics, their first real challenge to the established political order, had proven a costly and dismal failure.

Expelled from Jordan (which in a sense was their only natural habitat), the Palestinians almost instinctively moved en masse to Lebanon. Indeed, by 1969 the Palestinians had established a quasi-independent political and military entity in the porous and fragile confessional state; and in the same year the Lebanese army had clashed with Palestinian units, an engagement that had led to considerable Palestinian losses. It was thus inevitable that the presence of thousands of fully armed guerrillas in Lebanon in the wake of the Jordanian civil war would push the communal and sectarian tensions to the breaking point.

Tension was exacerbated by Israel's policy of instant and punitive retaliation against Palestinian concentrations inside Lebanon. The hostility of the anti-Palestinian Lebanese, mostly Maronite Christians, grew with every Israeli air raid on Lebanese territory. In contrast, most Lebanese Muslims supported, or at least acquiesced in, the Palestinian presence either because of ideological and religious affinity or because they felt that with the influx of thousands of well-armed Palestinian fighters they would be able to tilt the domestic balance of power in their favor.

The Christian, primarily Maronite, concern over the Palestinian presence and activities was the natural response of a community that benefited most from the status quo and did not want to see it changed. After all, since the conclusion of the National Pact in 1943, the Christians had dominated the country politically, socially and economically. Now they could see their dominance being threatened by the Palestinian influx. In the first place, they resented this blatant infringement of Lebanese sovereignty. Second, they saw the Palestinians as a Trojan horse which would allow such radical Arab countries as Syria, Iraq and Libya to interfere in Lebanese domestic politics, thus making Lebanon the arena where inter-Arab conflicts and quarrels would be fought out. Third, they feared the inevitable change in the domestic balance of power, particularly as the Palestinians made common cause with a variety of leftist, primarily Muslim, groups that were joined in an organization called the National Movement under the leadership of an eccentric yet determined Druze feudal lord named Kamal Jumblatt.

By 1974–75, the political, and more importantly attitudinal, polarization between the antagonistic communities had assumed a rigidity which boded ill for Lebanon's future stability. Indeed, a domestic cold war had taken over social and political relations, and it only required a single incident for cold war to be transformed into full-fledged civil war. On Sunday, April 13, 1975, unidentified gunmen killed four members of the Maronite-Christian militia, the Phalange, whereupon a busload of Palestinians was ambushed by the Phalange and all its passengers murdered. The carnage of Lebanon's civil war had begun, and the Palestinians, wittingly or unwittingly, were to play a leading role in the unfolding, hideous drama.

I use the word "unwittingly" because Palestinians countered that they had neither ignited nor encouraged the eruption of violence in Lebanon; that they had never sought to overthrow or disturb the established political and social order. Even were it true, their denial is meaningless. Lebanon's social and religious balance was so delicate, so fragile, that there was no way it could sustain the influx of thousands of highly politicized, determined and armed Palestinians. In any case, even if they had decided to be law-abiding, the tendency of the Palestinians to create their own, almost independent political and social infrastructure, literally a state within a state, was bound to be seen as an encroachment on the sovereignty of the host nation—especially the dominant political and social groups, who naturally would be the greatest defenders of the status quo.

The Palestinians' radical role in Lebanon lasted throughout the Lebanese civil war until their expulsion from Lebanon, first by the Israelis in August 1982, and then by the Syrians in December 1983. Shortly after the beginning of the civil war, and despite PLO official policy not to interfere in Lebanon's domestic conflict, Palestinian groups, particularly the smaller leftist, non-Fateh organizations, became increasingly active on the side of the Muslim forces in Lebanon. Indeed, when in January 1976 the Maronite forces besieged the three Palestinian refugee camps of Tel al-Za'atar, Jisr al-Basha, and al-Dubbaya and then proceeded to overrun large Muslim neighborhoods in predominantly Christian East Beirut and to expel their inhabitants, it was units of the Palestinian Liberation Army (PLA), sent across the border from Syria, which stopped the Christian advance, imposing a temporary cease-fire. By then the PLO, including al-Fateh, was in full political and military alliance with Jumblatt's leftist, primarily Muslim, Lebanese National Movement.

It was this alliance which was to turn Syria, hitherto the unquestionable patron of the Palestinians, against Arafat and the PLO. Jumblatt, seizing the favorable configuration of forces in the wake of the PLA intervention, began to advocate and work for the complete defeat of the status quo. Fearful of the possibility of an Israeli intervention, the Syrians argued that such a solution would partition the country, turning the resultant Christian enclave into an Israeli client. Such an eventuality, which would dangerously undermine Syrian strategic and political interests, was totally unacceptable to the Damascus government. Arafat, torn between the perceived necessity of Syrian patronage and the intricate de facto alliance he had by then established with the National Movement, was racked by indecision but continued to fight alongside the National Movement. Thus, when the Syrian armed forces entered Lebanon in June 1976, they provided the strange spectacle of the self-declared "progressive" Arab state defending "rightist" Maronite Christians against the "revolutionary" designs of "radical" Palestinians.

Summarily and ruthlessly defeated by the Syrians, Arafat was made to learn the required lesson: that for his own and his movement's survival, he had to be particularly sensitive, even subservient, to Syria's interests. Any Palestinian leader, himself included, who tried to escape this straitjacket did so at his peril. Syria's presence in Lebanon and its control over competitive Palestinian groups was so pervasive that for the next six years Arafat, no doubt reluctantly, toed the Syrian line. In effect, during those years, the tenets of Palestinian radicalism became almost indistinguishable from Syria's overall strategy in Lebanon and in the Arab world. To make certain that the PLO chairman would have no excuses for pursuing even the semblance of an independent policy, Syria "invited" the Palestinian National Council, the highest executive authority whose resolutions could be used by Arafat as the pretext for an independent line, to hold its fourteenth and fifteenth sessions in 1979 and 1981 in Damascus under the vigilant eyes of the Syrian regime.

Here, I concede that the preceeding analysis simplifies a much more complex reality, for the Syrians, not unlike the Palestinians, were themselves sucked into the quagmire of Lebanese politics. With every passing day, Syria's political and military involvement in Lebanon mounted, and its freedom of maneuverability decreased. Once the Palestinians were taught not to contravene

Syria's political and strategic dictates, Syria (as explained in Chapter 4) could not but revert to its wholehearted defense of the Palestinian resistance. First vis-à-vis the Christian Maronite forces, increasingly supported by the Israelis, then against Israel itself, and finally even against American threats, Syria itself was becoming almost a prisoner of Palestinian radicalism. Many Syrians at the time were becoming concerned that Palestinian "irresponsibility" and "anarchical" behavior would push Syria into a premature confrontation with Israel.[3] In a sense, therefore, Syria and the PLO adhered to each other's interests not so much because of clear and congruous definitions of political and strategic goals, but because the situation in Lebanon during that period fused, almost inevitably, the two positions together.

Consequently, Palestinian power during 1976–82 grew considerably. There were three major concentrations of Palestinian presence and activism. Around Tripoli in the north, they were among a friendly Sunni population highly sympathetic to their cause—a population relatively untouched by Israeli vengeance because of its distance from the Israeli border. In the Lebanese capital, battling the pro-Israeli Maronite Christians of East Beirut, the Palestinians were entrenched in Muslim West Beirut, allied mainly with Lebanese leftist and Sunni groups such as the Communist Party and al-Murabitoun, but increasingly at odds with the Shiite immigrants from South Lebanon. In the south the Palestinians faced their most difficult task. They were subjected to the full fury of Israel's retaliatory action. Additionally, and more damaging to the Palestinian cause, the PLO fighters gradually lost the support of the primarily Shiite population of southern Lebanon. The latter not only blamed Israel's massive devastation of their land on the Palestinians, but also resented the Palestinians' military control of the region and their seemingly total insensitivity to its inhabitants' concerns. Friction between Palestinians and Shiites grew so that by the beginning of the 1980s clashes between the two communities had become almost a regular occurrence.

It was hardly surprising that when the Israelis invaded Lebanon, the Shiites acted with measured indifference and in some instances with obvious glee. And Israel was supported in cleansing the area of the Palestinian military presence. But Israeli objectives were much broader than first anticipated. Jerusalem sought the complete expulsion of the Palestinians from Lebanon and the simultaneous defeat of the Syrian army so that pro-Israeli Maronite political and military hegemony over Lebanon could be ensured. On this last goal, the Israelis were to be bitterly disappointed, but they did defeat the Syrians and, more importantly, they did expel the Palestinians from the south and from Beirut.

The departure of Palestinian fighters from Beirut in August 1982 marked a turning point in PLO strategy. No longer able to wage a military struggle against the Israelis and having tasted the full venom of Israel's power, the mainstream core of the PLO began exploring the feasibility of non-military options. Paradoxically, it was the Israeli-induced Palestinian expulsion from Lebanon that freed Arafat from Lebanon's quagmire and Syrian domination. At this juncture, the radical orientation of mainstream Palestinian activity sharply declined.

Throughout 1983 Arafat endeavored to improve and cement PLO relations with other Arab governments. After all, since the early, highly ideological days of the late 1960s, the leaders of the mainstream PLO had quietly discarded the goal of transforming the Arab political order, which some of its more radical elements had so dearly cherished. Needing the financial and political support of Arab governments, each constituent member of the PLO quickly found a patron. And, outside of the mainstream PLO, it had become pathetically obvious that, in many instances, a subversive act or militant invective by a Palestinian group against an Arab government or another Palestinian organization was hardly a manifestation of the group's radical ideology, but more often a service paid to the patron. This was particularly characteristic of the smaller groups, the most notorious of which was the organization led by the mysterious and seemingly psychotic Abu Nidhal.

Because of its size and centrality, on the other hand, al-Fateh dominated the organizational structure of the PLO and thus, in a sense, was bound to become the most institutionalized group within the PLO. Throughout the 1970s al-Fateh had not advocated the overthrow of Arab regimes as part of its radical ideology. Consequently, the PLO's estimated annual budget in the early 1980s of $500 million, the bulk of which came from Arab governments, owed much to the good relations that al-Fateh and its leaders had established with various Arab regimes on behalf of the PLO.

After his expulsion from Beirut in 1982, Arafat and his mainstream PLO proceeded to concentrate their efforts more on diplomacy and less on armed struggle. Naturally he sought the support of the conservative, status quo Arab governments, particularly Egypt and Jordan—the two states, along with Iraq, toward which Syria was hostile. In response, the Damascus regime engineered a revolt against Arafat from within the Fateh ranks in October 1983, as a result of which intra-Palestinian battles near Tripoli in northern Lebanon erupted. During a month of intermittent fighting, the rebels, backed by the Syrians, were able to compel yet another ignominious expulsion of Arafat and 4,000 of his loyalists.

If Arafat had any doubts about his new orientation, these were dispelled after the Tripoli events. Two days after his expulsion, the PLO chairman held an unscheduled two-hour meeting with President Mubarak of Egypt, leader of the only Arab country that had a peace treaty with Israel. Two days later, for the first time in almost two decades of revolutionary struggle, Arafat said that "it was time to begin thinking about the creation of a Palestinian government-in-exile."[4] It was clear that Arafat was quickly, and seemingly irrevocably, changing course. And he could do this because the Tripoli events seem to have freed him psychologically from the suffocating patronage of the Syrian regime: three weeks before his humiliating departure from Tripoli, he had criticized "the Syrian regime and its gangsters"[5] for their support of rebel forces, and had accepted an offer from King Hussein of Jordan to return to Amman and resume Palestinian-Jordanian talks.

PLO activity during 1984 and 1985 clearly shows that the mainstream core of the organization, still with a massive numerical preponderance and claiming by far the greatest support among the Palestinian population, had lost much of its earlier commitment to revolutionary goals and methods. Set against al-Fateh and its policies were the two radical organizations of the neo-Marxist National Alliance and the Syrian-backed Democratic Alliance. The radical challenge in fact speeded up al-Fateh's efforts to put its house in order, particularly after dissident factions had torpedoed the agreement Arafat had reached with King Hussein in April 1984. After an initial postponement of the PNC meeting, the Fateh central committee, disregarding its commitment to Palestinian consensus, met in October 1984 and decided that henceforth al-Fateh "would run the organization in its own way, with or without the smaller groups"; that the PNC would convene by the end of November; "that it was the 'national duty' of Palestinians to attend"; and that the minority had to "accept the decision of the majority."[6] The pro-Syrian radical opposition groups, who themselves were simultaneously meeting in Damascus, predicted that most PNC members would boycott the scheduled Amman meeting, and then, for good measure, threatened to blow up the house of anyone who dared to undermine that prediction.

In the event, the PNC did meet in Amman in November, and a majority did attend. The Congress re-elected Arafat unanimously to the chairmanship; it expelled from the PNC one of Arafat's bitterest critics, Ahmad Jibril, the leader of the ultra-militant Popular Front for the Liberation of Palestine-General Command (PFLP-GC); it delegated Arafat "to strengthen ties [with Jordan] and coordinate efforts for joint action to regain Palestinian and Arab lands"; and it endorsed his visit to Egypt "as a step toward strengthening relations between the Palestinian and Egyptian people."[7] Armed with the legitimacy of PNC approval, the chairman of the PLO was set to steer the organization, once the epitome of the Arab radical creed, onto a diplomatic, less radical path.

This was by no means an easy road. Arafat needed to prove to his public that diplomacy, pragmatism and moderation produce results; he needed to succeed, and he could not wait forever to do it. Yet he had to contend with a number of difficult, almost insurmountable, obstacles. He had to convince long-standing and powerful colleagues within al-Fateh to put their reputations, even lives, on the line and joint him on a risky (some would call it "reckless") diplomatic journey that had no guarantees for the ultimate achievement of Palestinian aspirations. He had to deal with a partner in King Hussein who, for all his public deference to Palestinian sovereignty, could not realistically relish the prospect of a West Bank Palestinian state neighboring on an East Bank Hashemite Kingdom, the majority of whose population is Palestinian. Arafat was also faced with a hostile and suspicious Israel, which, in any case, was reluctant to even consider the prospect of giving up the West Bank.

As though this were not enough of a concern, the Palestinian dissidents, the radical elements, particularly those under Syrian control, constantly endeavored to undermine Arafat's legitimacy, based on decades of promises of deliverance through revolutionary action, by labeling his efforts to seek political solutions to the Palestinian plight as "capitulationist," and projecting themselves as the true heirs to the PLO's revolutionary tradition. If this were not enough, the dissidents, seemingly encouraged by Damascus, tried to dilute the chairman's support by striking terror into his followers' hearts. A month after his election at the PNC meeting to the Executive Committee of the PLO, Fahed Qawesmeh, the Israeli-expelled ex-mayor of Hebron, was assassinated outside his home in Amman. His murder on December 29, 1984, followed an appearance a day earlier on Syrian television by the displaced speaker of the PNC, Khalid Fahoum, in which he vehemently denounced Mr. Qawasmeh. However, it must have been a source of great reassurance for the PLO chairman when much of the West Bank closed for a one-day strike to protest the assassination. Even so, although almost completely lacking in popular support, Arafat's enemies were backed by a vigorous and powerful radical Arab state, determined to keep the Palestinian movement totally in its grip. Formidable obstacles, internal to and external of the PLO, were thus bound to make Arafat's diplomatic road perhaps his riskiest gamble to date.

Religious Radicalism

Radical religious fundamentalism filled the revolutionary void and emerged as the primary challenge to state stability and regime survival in the Arab world at a time of crisis for the Palestinian movement and Arab nationalism. It was the time when the Palestinian movement was being ruthlessly cut down to size by Syria in Lebanon in 1976 and after. Palestinian leaders were learning yet again that, no matter how sophisticated an institutional structure or powerful a military machine they were able to build, they still were no match for the organized and overwhelming violence a state could unleash. It was a time when the spirit of the secularist radicals, first through the defeat of revolutionary Arab nationalism and then through the agony of the Palestinian struggle, seemed to have been finally broken by the power of states as disparate as Israel, Jordan and Syria. Moreover it was a time when regimes and political leaders could celebrate their tenth anniversary in power, whereas before, for some, a year or two in power had been considered a commendable feat.

I do not mean to imply that prior to the late 1970s there had been no religious challenge to the authority of the state. To be sure, there was; but its potency, both objectively and in the eyes of those whom it challenged, took a mammoth qualitative leap in the late 1970s. The reasons are several. Until the early 1970s religious radicalism had to compete first with a buoyant and secularist Arab nationalism and then, after 1967, with a Palestinian liberation movement, which by virtue of some successful and dramatic acts had been able for a few years to capture peoples' hearts and monopolize their attention. When the infatuation between the PLO and the Arab masses began to fade in the early 1970s, two Arab states mounted their best military effort to date against the Israelis, immediately followed by concerted Arab economic action against the Western world, and the people began to have faith again in the probity and competence of their rulers. President Sadat of Egypt, for instance, was able for a few years to rest his credibility on the catch phrase al-Ubur (the crossing), constantly reminding his people that it was his courage, his vision and his intelligent leadership that led to the Egyptian crossing of the Suez Canal in October 1973. Four or five years later—when the novelty had worn off; when regimes, with few exceptions, had not been able to build on the good will of 1973–74; when corruption, economic mismanagement and bureaucratic inefficiency continued to be the order of the day—to mount a challenge to the state's authority was no longer a daunting prospect.

In the second half of the 1970s radical religious groups became more prominent, more active and more adventurous. If a spur was needed to finally shift them from the wings to center stage of radical political activity in the Arab world, it was provided by the Iranian revolution of 1978–79. Here was the irrefutable proof of what Muslims could achieve if they allowed their faith to guide their political goals and action. Here was a live demonstration of the power of Islam to put Islam in power. And when the Shah, America's much vaunted ally, the pillar of stability in the region, was finally hounded out of his country by millions of fist-clenching Shiite zealots, Iran became the model and inspiration for radical Muslim activists in the Arab world. During the revolutionary euphoria of those early days of the Iranian revolution, ethnic differences between Arab and Persian figured little in the consciousness of Muslim Arabs, and Sunni-Shiite doctrinal disagreements seemed to matter even less. What was relevant was the sight of an old, frail cleric toppling a powerful American-backed monarchy and proclaiming the establishment of a clergy-led Islamic state.

The late 1970s, therefore, saw the Muslim radical groups formulate goals and take actions that were far more ambitious and daring than in earlier periods. In Egypt, the Muslim Brotherhood organization had been clandestinely active against the government of the day since the 1930s. In 1948 it assassinated the Prime Minister, Nuqrashi Pasha; and in 1954 it mounted an unsuccessful attempt on the life of Abd al-Nasser. Then in 1965 Nasser's security uncovered a widespread plot engineered by the Brotherhood under Sayyid Qutb's charismatic leadership. Thousands were arrested, hundreds were jailed, and Qutb and two other leaders were hanged. In the 1970s, the Brotherhood's revolutionary activities declined perceptibly, partly because of the lack of an inspirational leader, and partly because President Sadat tried to co-opt the Brothers into his political system in an effort to counteract the leftist supporters of his predecessor, Abd al-Nasser.

The Brotherhood's gradual institutionalization meant, however, that splinter groups would take up the radical struggle. In April 1974 a Muslim organization called al-Tahrir al-Islami (Islamic Liberation) attacked the Technical Military Academy in a suburb of Cairo, and in a pitched battle between the attackers and the academy's guards, 11 persons were killed and 27 wounded. The group's leader, Salih Sirriya, had opposed the attack, citing Sadat's popularity in the wake of the 1973 October war, but he had been overruled by the organization's executive council. The operational plan was first to seize the academy and then go to the headquarters of the Arab Socialist Union (at that time Egypt's only political party), where President Sadat had been scheduled to deliver a major speech; Sadat would be arrested, along with senior party officials, after which Sirriya would go on the air to proclaim the overthrow of Sadat and the establishment of a genuine Islamic state. But, to have ever thought of overthrowing the government at a time when it was at the height of its popularity was an act of self-delusion. Needless to say, the coup attempt failed, hundreds of Muslim militants were arrested, and Sirriya was executed.

The arrests uncovered other Islamic groups that were working separately for the establishment of an Islamic state. One, al-Takfir wal-Higra, in 1977, kidnapped a former minister of religious endowments, who allegedly had been a sympathizer in the past, but who later had issued a *fatwa* (religious ruling) against the organization. The kidnappers demanded not only the release of their brethren from prison, but also a public announcement by the government, to be broadcast over the radio, that Egypt would henceforth be governed in strict accordance with Islamic principles. These demands were rejected, as a result of which the ex-minister was killed. Ruthlessly pursuing the membership of the organization, the government arrested over 400 active members and sympathizers and five leaders were executed.

A second group which had its roots in the 1974 abortive attack on the military technical academy was destined to achieve a dramatic success. On October 6, 1981, the Tanzim al-Gihad (Holy War Organization) group assassinated President Sadat in an attack mounted during a military parade in Cairo. Taking advantage of the ensuing confusion in the country, the group engineered a mini-insurrection in the town of Assyut in Upper Egypt, when its members attacked and occupied the police headquarters. Only after considerable reinforcement by the security forces and a bloody confrontation in which over 50 people were killed and more than a hundred wounded, was the government able to restore order. The scope of the operations, their ferocity, and ultimately their relative success no doubt could be explained by a number of factors, but it can hardly go unnoticed that the Tanzim operations occurred in 1981 and that its organizational structure, according to its leader in Assyut, was created in January 1980, a time when fascination with Iran's Islamic republic was at its height.[8]

The primary method in which the state has responded to these radical groups has been through determined coercion. Security forces have engaged in pitched battles with Muslim radicals, hundreds have been arrested and jailed, and leaders have been executed. However, Sadat and later Mubarak have also tried to isolate the extremists by co-opting the more moderate Islamicists into the political process, as well as by projecting an image of themselves as pious Muslims.

Soon after he assumed the presidency, Sadat made al-Sharia, the holy Islamic law, *a* source of legislation; but in 1980, with the increased buoyancy of the Islamic opposition groups, Sadat used a plebiscite to make al-Sharia *the main* source of legislation. Sadat also brought back from exile in Saudi Arabia two Brotherhood leaders, Umar Tilmisani and Said Ramadhan, and though the Brotherhood continued to be officially banned, Ramadhan was allowed to assume the unofficial leadership of nine deputies, known for their Brotherhood sympathies, in the national assembly. On a personal level, Sadat projected an image of piety and strict adherence to Islamic precepts, and his speeches and official declarations were interspersed with frequent Koranic quotations. Sadat's problem was that he also had another, vastly contradictory, image: the darling of the Western media; the man who was surrounded by affluent and corrupt men; the husband of a highly visible and assertive woman, seemingly more attuned to Western than to Islamic culture; the loyal friend of America, Israel and the Shah. By 1981, only the traditionally obsequious Ulema of al-Azhar were supporters of Sadat; the rest of the Islamicists, even the moderate wing of the Brotherhood, had become totally alienated from Egypt's "Shah." Realizing this, Sadat reverted to an iron-fist policy. In September 1981, he arrested over 2,000 people, mostly Islamicists that included the Brotherhood's Tilmisani, and nationalized all private mosques. He threatened more arrests, but it was too late. A month later he was assassinated.

Mubarak has followed a similar two-tier policy. He has not shirked from a determined, ruthless suppression of anti-government activists. But he has also tried to continue the co-optation of the Islamic movement into the political process. He released Tilmisani from detention and enlisted his support in combating the radicals. He launched an official Islamic weekly magazine, *al-Liwa al-Islami,* in which some Muslim critics of the government were allowed to air their views. And in the general elections of 1984, the Brotherhood's alliance with the conservative yet secular New Wafd Party was tacitly accepted, even approved, by the government. In all this, and notwithstanding a general economic collapse, the Islamic radical threat to Mubarak's political order seems less potent than it was in the latter years of Sadat's rule. Apart from more general regional factors (analyzed in the concluding chapter), one specific reason for this could be Mubarak's lifestyle, which, in contrast to that of Sadat, is simple and low-key, devoid of conspicuous opulence, and untainted by signs of corruption.

The history of Islamic radical activity in Syria during the 1970s and 1980s is not too dissimilar from the Egyptian experience. There certainly was continuing opposition to Assad's Baathist/Alawi political order in the first half of the 1970s, the most serious of which occurred in 1973 following the introduction of the new secularist Syrian Constitution. Leaders of the Sunni Muslim Brotherhood urged their followers to protest against the Constitution. Riots soon spread from the most conservative, Sunni-dominated towns of Hama and Homs to Aleppo and Damascus. The rioters demanded the inclusion of a provision pertaining to the status of Islam as the official religion of the state. Slogans such as "Islam is our constitution" and "there is no leader but Muhammad" were brandished. While the regime used harsh and suppressive measures to quell the violence, Assad also compromised by modifying the Constitution to include a stipulation that the President must be an adherent of the Islamic faith. Moreover, the Alawi President spared no effort to minimize the Sunni-Alawi distinction, especially by encouraging Sunni Ulema to declare that the Alawi sect was an integral part of Islam.

As in Egypt, however, the ferocity of the Islamic resistance to the regime increased considerably in the latter years of the 1970s. While the general transformation of the Arab radical milieu outlined earlier in this chapter was in part responsible for heightened Islamic radicalism, Syria's military intervention in Lebanon on the side of the Maronites against the Muslim/Palestinian forces was particularly galling to the Muslim activists. Assad's apparent pride in reaffirming the secularist principles which had guided Syria's intervention in Lebanon only added to the anger and contempt of the Muslim radicals, and his declaration that "religion is for God and the homeland is for all"[9] was an assertion that would be considered by a true Muslim believer as bordering on blasphemy.

Moreover, as Syria was gradually sucked into Lebanon's quagmire and the intervention was slowly becoming Assad's own Vietnam, the President began to depend more on his own community for political survival. It was inevitable that the corrupt and intensely disliked and feared brother of the president, Rifaat, the commander of Siraya al-Difai', the impeccably trained and equipped Alawi praetorian guard, would be pushed to the forefront of public attention. Consequently, the damaging perception of the Assad regime as blatantly sectarian, wholly dependent on coercion ruthlessly conducted by members of its minority sect, became more current among the majority of the Sunni population. This in turn provided the Muslim radicals, all of whom were Sunni, with a friendlier environment for their operation.

Armed resistance began in earnest in 1977 with selective assassinations of Alawi officials. A dramatic escalation occurred in 1979 with the murder of 32 and the wounding of 54 Alawi artillery cadets in Aleppo and other daring attacks on government installations and armed confrontations with security forces. The regime responded by intensifying its own ruthless pursuit of the Muslim opposition and by making membership in, even association with, the Brotherhood punishable by death. It is no exaggeration to say that the confrontation between the Islamic radicals and the regime during 1979–82 approximated an armed insurrection.

The climax came, as it was bound to do, in the fiercely conservative Sunni city of Hama on the night of February 3, 1982, when the population was awakened by a call to arms and told that the city had been liberated by the Muslim Brothers from the control of the Assad regime. Over 500 Muslim militants, armed with automatic rifles, machine guns, even shoulder-fired rocket launchers, had attacked and in some cases occupied police headquarters, party offices and army barracks. Some "250 so-called atheists, or known supporters of the regime, were summarily executed."[10] Muslim radicals then placed themselves in strategic positions, primarily in the heavily populated bazaar section of the city. There can be little doubt that the Brotherhood's goal was to engage the regime long enough for a major revolution to occur. The government knew that too. Thus, during three weeks of utmost savagery that included heavy and indiscriminate bombardment by aircraft and land-based artillery, thousands of people were killed and almost half of the city was razed to the ground by Rifaat's Alawi forces and loyal Baathist militia. No one, not even the Syrian leadership, suggests that the Organization is dead. But the blow was such, that for a number of

years after the Hama "incidents" hardly a sound, not even a mur-
mur of protest, had come from the Muslim radicals in Syria.

The Damascus government had decided, successfully as far as
one can tell, to depend primarily on brutal coercion in its fight
against Islamic radicalism. No less brutal has been President Hussein's response to the Shiite al-Da'wa party. Earlier encounters between the party and the government had been characterized by
firm government reprisals. Thus, when in 1977 a Shiite mourning
procession between the two holy Shiite cities of Najaf and Karbala
turned into a furious anti-government demonstration, the Baathist
regime made widespread arrests, put many of those arrested on
trial and executed some of them. The real escalation, however, occurred after 1978 with the gradual collapse of the Pahlavi order and
the advent of the Islamic revolution in Iran, and the realization by
one and all that the only other Muslim country with an indigenous
Shiite majority was neighboring Iraq.

Taking heart from the momentous happenings across the border and anticipating moral and material support from a revolutionary government that had explicitly rejected the concept of borders
within the Islamic world, the clandestinely organized Iraqi Shiite al-
Da'wa party abruptly escalated its anti-government activities.
Throughout 1979 the party engineered a series of demonstrations,
anti-government agitation, and attacks on government buildings
mainly in Shiite-dominated southern Iraq. More ominously for the
regime, the leader of al-Da'wa, the charismatic and universally respected Shiite cleric, Imam Baqir al-Sadr, endorsed without reser-
vation the Iranian revolution and the concept of *wilayat al-faqih*
(rule of the Jurist), which, on philosophical grounds, would render
the Baathist government in Baghdad theoretically illegal. To repeat,
whether al-Sadr was referring to an "ideal state of affairs" which
exists in theory, or whether he actually saw an operational dimension to the concept in the Iraqi situation is unclear. What is clear is
that both the government and members of the party believed that
al-Sadr was committed to creating a Khomeini-like Shiite political
order in Iraq.

In April 1980, members of al-Da'wa threw a bomb at Tariq
Aziz, the only Christian member of the Iraqi leadership, while he
was addressing a university rally. He escaped with slight injuries,
but two students were killed. In the funeral procession three days

later, another grenade was thrown by al-Da'wa members which killed one person. In the same month, a number of attacks against official Iraqi targets inside and outside Iraq were mounted by members of the party. Saddam Hussein, ruthless and resolute, ordered the execution of al-Sadr and his activist sister and embarked upon not only the brutal suppression of the party but also the mass expulsion of some 35,000 Iraqi Shiites, supposedly of Iranian descent.

Along with the stick, Hussein offered a carrot. During 1979 he accelerated the implementation of various social welfare programs aimed at the poor, the majority of whom were Shiite. The government also worked on improving housing, education and medical services in areas of high Shiite concentration. Government funding for Shiite holy places was significantly raised after 1979. Thus, in 1982, for example, $48 million was allocated to the Shiite holy cities of Najaf and Karbala. In Najaf, the inner shrine of al-Haydariya mosque was lavishly ornamented with gold and silver leaf, and in Karbala mosques were installed with power generators and air-conditioning in addition to marble work and crystal chandeliers. Moreover, Hussein began to refer frequently and reverently to the early leaders of Shiite Islam, Ali and Hussein. In one address, he declared: "our great ancestor, the Father of all martyrs, Hussein, may God's peace be upon him, stands as a lofty symbol of heroism, glory, firmness in defending right." He extolled "the holy land of Iraq which harbors the remains of our ancestor Ali, may God brighten his face."[11] Simultaneously, however, he showed his singleminded ruthlessness when, in 1984, he had six members of a leading Shiite religious family from Najaf, al-Hakims, executed in retaliation for speeches made by the cleric Muhammed Baqir al-Hakim, who heads an "Iraqi government in exile" in Tehran. This stick-and-carrot policy, plus the loss of the charismatic Imam Baqir al-Sadr, contributed to a considerable decline in the fortunes of al-Da'wa, so that in 1985 the party was a shadow of its former self during the euphoric days of 1979.

Khomeini's assumption of power in 1979 also had an uplifting effect on the Shiite population of South Lebanon. By 1980 Amal would boast more than 4,000 determined fighters, and in those days Amal's primary struggle was against the PLO. Shiite resentment of the Palestinian guerrillas had grown not only because it was the Shiites who became the primary victims of repeated Israeli attacks prompted by the Palestinian presence, but also because of the Palestinians' harsh and inconsiderate treatment of villagers. Just before his disappearance in Libya, Amal's political and religious leader, Imam Musa al-Sadr, had articulated Shiite resentment and mounting contempt of the Palestinians:

> The Palestinian Resistance is not a revolution; it does not seek martyrdom. It is a military machine that terrorizes the Arab world. With weapons Arafat gets money; with money he can feed the press; and thanks to the press he can get a hearing before world public opinion. . . . The Shia have finally gotten over their inferiority complex vis-à-vis the Palestinian organizations.[12]

Clashes with the Shiites were proving to be increasingly costly for the Palestinians. But, stubborn as always, the Palestinian fighters were in no mood to compromise, in no hurry to meet the Shiites half-way. Plagued by corrupt and insensitive regional leadership, and obsessed with the righteousness of their own cause to the exclusion of other concerns, the Palestinians could not change their ways. The Shiites, thus, were bound to escalate their conflict with their "former allies," but still were not strong enough to mount a serious challenge to the powerful Palestinian presence. It needed the Israelis to render them that service.

Israel's expulsion of the PLO from Lebanon in late summer 1982 cleared the decks for the various sectarian groups in Lebanon to make their bids for power. The one million Shiites, the largest community in Lebanon, brandishing a new assertiveness through a militia which had grown to over 30,000 committed fighters, were no longer willing to be castaways in the impoverished Jabal Amil. Nabih Berri, to the best of his ability, tried to explain the new political realities of Lebanon to the status quo men who had ruled Lebanon for four decades. But the Maronites, having for years blamed all Lebanon's ills on the Palestinian presence, saw in the PLO departure a chance to revive the old Maronite-Sunni proportioning of political power that would reinstate and reaffirm the political and social status quo.

That might have been a delusion, but in the context of the times it looked quite feasible. The Sunnis would readily accept, since they had no military power to speak of, and in any case their status prior to the civil war was second only to the Maronites. The Druze, fierce fighters that they were, were after all a small minority that was able to offer substantial resistance primarily because of Syrian materiel and logistical support, and while that was certainly a problem before June 1982, the Israelis were now expected to effectively neutralize the Syrian presence. And the new demographic and military power of the Shiites had not yet registered. The Shiites, it seems, were still considered a submissive and downtrodden community of peasants that did not care about, and consequently could not participate in, political power games.

Israel and the United States, for different reasons, accepted this scenario, and proceeded to help achieve Maronite hegemony. At this juncture, the Shiite fight was no longer confined to Lebanon, but took on a transnational character. It was hardly surprising that the Shiite groups which took the struggle against the Americans and Israelis most to heart were the smaller dissident groups, more committed than Amal to the concept of a Shiite theocratic state, and consequently more susceptible to the symbols and slogans of the Islamic revolution in Iran. The year 1983 saw a kind of division of labor within the Shiite radical groups: Amal, allying itself with Druze militia, concentrated on fighting the government of Amin Gemayel, its Phalangist militia, and its newly formed army, trained and lavishly equipped by the Americans. The smaller, religiously fanatical groups like Hizbollah and Islamic Jihad, on the other hand, turned their attention to the Americans and Israelis.

The Israelis, in particular, had lost a golden opportunity to achieve their age-old objective of ensuring the security of their northern border. Had they treated the Shiite population with respect and sensitivity, had they capitalized on the good will generated by Israel's expulsion of the Palestinians from the south, had they then entrusted the security of southern Lebanon to the Shiites, whose hostility toward the Palestinians probably equalled that of the Israelis themselves, Israel might well have achieved a security arrangement that would have precluded the immense cost in loss of life, demoralization, and cynicism subsequently endured by its armed forces.

But the Israelis, who spent so much time since the establishment of their state perfecting the science of war, had woefully neglected to refine their skills at the art of peace. For the Israelis, breaking their enemies' spirits through overwhelming military power had become such an easy option that they seemingly lost the ability or the inclination to reach out and try to win their hearts. As Israel's occupation grew longer and its ways harsher, Shiite resistance correspondingly escalated. Rather than accommodating the villagers, Israel left the security of the region to its client militia of Major Saad Haddad. And there was the United States, fully and actively supportive of the Maronite minority political order in Beirut and of Israel's demands and activities in the south. Thus, in the eyes of the Shiites, the political status quo as it existed in 1983 was represented by the alliance of the Maronites, Israel and the United States.

The first major radical act (less consequential acts had already taken place) against the status quo occurred on April 18, 1983, when a bomb exploded at the United States Embassy in Beirut, killing 63 people and injuring close to 100 and completely destroying the central consular section of the building. Seventeen of those killed were American nationals, including marine guards, senior embassy staff, and the director of the CIA's office for the Near East and South Asia, along with six other CIA personnel.

The handwriting was on the wall not only for the Americans but also for the Israelis. Throughout the summer and autumn of 1983, Amal was gradually diverting its attention back to the south. Along with, but independently of, the more militant Shiite groups, a series of quick hit-and-run guerrilla attacks were mounted against the Israelis which steadily added to the casualty figures of Israel's occupying army. Similar attacks were also directed by Amal and the other groups at the American, French and Italian members of the international peace-keeping force in Beirut. With increasing violence against their forces, the Israelis retaliated with further oppressive measures in the south, and the Americans decided to intervene directly on the side of the Maronites in the domestic conflict. An explosion was waiting to happen.

On October 23, 1983, a suicide truck loaded with an estimated 5,000 pounds of explosives crashed through the headquarters of the U.S. Marine battalion in Beirut. When the carnage had finally been cleared, Washington was stunned to learn that 241 marines had lost their lives. An identical attack on the French quarters, which killed 58 soldiers, suggested that Hussein Musawi and his Islamic Jihad, Iran's most faithful ally in Lebanon, were guilty of both attacks for singling out the French could only have been because of France's support for Iraq in its war with Iran.

Seven days earlier, an Israeli convoy, epitomizing all the characteristics of Israel's occupation, had forcibly pushed its way through a religious procession in Nabatiya commemorating the most revered day in Shiite Islam. In the ensuing rage, two persons were killed and several injured. The fanatical martyrs were ready. Less than three weeks after the incident, a suicidal car-bomb attack against Israeli headquarters in Tyre killed 61 people of whom 28 were Israeli soldiers. Islamic Jihad claimed responsibility and declared that it was prepared to send 2,000 fighters "to die in South Lebanon in order to expel the Zionist enemy."[13]

While all this terror was bound to have an impact on the calculations of the Americans, Israelis and Maronites, the one event that finally led to the collapse of the status quo in Lebanon occurred in the first five days of February 1984 when Amal, supported by Druze militia, stormed into Beirut, fought a successful battle against the Lebanese army and irregular Phalangist forces, and ended up in control of West Beirut. Shiite soldiers answered Berri's call for them to desert, and the Lebanese army, the symbol of a year-long American endeavor, disintegrated in three days. And its collapse signaled the impending defeat of the status quo.

On February 5 the Lebanese cabinet that had found no place for Nabih Berri resigned. On February 18 Washington evacuated its marines from Beirut, thus indirectly admitting the failure of its policy. And on April 30 Berri joined the cabinet on the understanding that he would be allocated responsibility for the south of Lebanon. Nine months later, in January 1985, with its army under continuing and mounting harrassment by Amal and the other Shiite guerrilla groups, the Israeli cabinet voted to withdraw unilaterally and completely from Lebanon. In Shiite eyes, the three constituents of Lebanon's status quo of 1983, the Maronites, the United States and Israel, had disintegrated in utter disarray less than two years later.

Of all the religious radical groups, Amal seems to be the only success story. Even with the loss of a charismatic leader and the bickering that occurred among his inheritors, Amal was able to sustain itself, grow, and score notable victories. As I indicated earlier, it is perhaps the aura of success that breeds confidence in the cause and the leadership. If that is the case, then Amal was fortunate to have waged its struggle against a weak central authority that in the final analysis was dependent on an army torn by sectarian divisions, a militia smaller in number than that of the Shiites, and outside powers that had no real understanding of, or sensitivity to, Lebanon's special character. How truly envious of all this the religious radicals in Egypt, Syria and Iraq must be.

Part Four

Conclusion

7
The Fate of Arab Radicalism

The United States has exhibited intense distaste for and hostility toward rebellions and revolutions in the Middle East, considering them to be, on the whole, anti-Western. For example, Washington has unswervingly opposed the radical activities of Libya's Qadhafi and Syria's Assad, to say nothing of Iran's ayatollahs and the Islamic fundamentalist groups in the Arab world, Shiite or Sunni, which, without doubt, have been inspired by Tehran's feats. In a sense, this American position is easily understandable since, on balance, Middle Eastern radicalism in the 1980s has tended not to serve Western, particularly American, interests.

Standing against Western interests, however, does not mean that the radical Arab states and groups share either identical goals or common organizational and institutional networks. As I made clear in the first chapter, the Arab radicals are defined solely by their desire and efforts to undermine the Arab status quo order, and by their antipathy toward Israel and their seeming ambivalence to United States policies in the area. Beyond that, it is important to understand (especially in light of present American sentiments) that there is no ideologically and/or organizationally united radical movement, no tightly controlled radical conspiracy, no coherent or cohesive radical brotherhood.

Radical vengeance, in fact, has been frequently unleashed at the radicals themselves. The ferocity of Amal's fight against the Israelis in 1983–84 was more than matched by the organization's later conflict in summer 1985 with the PLO in Beirut. Indeed, Amal's own relations with its fellow Shiite radical groups, Islamic Jihad and Hizbollah, are hardly imbued with the fraternalism that is supposed to bind together the radical sons of Imams Ali and Hussein. In the battles that raged between Amal and the PLO in Lebanon in 1985 and 1986, Hizbollah fighters joined forces with the Palestinians against their Shiite brothers.[1] Moreover, those who argue that the Lebanese radicals ("terrorists" is the more commonly used word) are all controlled from Damascus either are blissfully ignorant of Lebanon's political quagmire or have a political axe to grind. True, Syria is the pre-eminent outside power in Lebanon today and, like other external parties, is actively involved in aiding materially and logistically its Lebanese allies, who at present seem to hold the upper hand. Syria has also discovered, however, that on many occasions, some crucial for its prestige and credibility in the area, its supposed clients have exhibited an independence of will that mirrors Syria's relations with its own patron, the Soviet Union.

The Syrian-"controlled" Palestinian guerrillas, for example, were instructed by Damascus to aid the Amal militia in their battle against the Arafat loyalists in Beirut in summer 1985. To the distinct embarrassment of the Syrians, however, a large number of these so-called pro-Syrian guerrillas ended up fighting alongside their Palestinian brothers. Even more difficult to influence, let alone control, have been the fundamentalist Shiite groups in Lebanon which have been described by Syria's foreign minister, Abd al-Halim Khaddam, as being "like stone in their hardness."[2] President Assad, in an interview in May 1986, articulated Syria's frustrations with the seeming impotence of its power:

> The situation in Lebanon is not a classic one, not only from the point of view of the absence of the state, but also as a result of the situation in the political parties in Lebanon. One cannot say that the leadership of each party has full disciplinary control over all the party followers. Besides, there is a big number of small groupings, and to deal with these small groupings is much more difficult than to deal with the bigger ones. And these small groupings are changeable and keep on the move, which adds to the difficulty of the problem. . . . Of course, we

have certain influence on the big political parties in Lebanon. In fact,
our influence on the smaller groups is limited. Yet, in normal conditions, one may find channels for dealing with them.[3]

Nor could the mainstream Amal organization be considered a
Syrian client. It is erroneously thought that it was Syria which secured the release of the TWA hostages in summer 1985. In fact,
what Syria secured was a promise by the United States that the
Shiite prisoners in Israel would be freed very shortly after the release of the TWA hostages. Additionally, the Syrians, in the classic
manner of third-party mediators, communicated to Nabih Berri,
Amal's leader—whose own credibility, even legitimacy, was on the
line—their assessment that this was the best deal that he could
hope to get. It was thus after evaluating his, and his organization's,
interests that Berri decided to let the American hostages leave
Beirut.

Disparate as it undoubtedly is, Arab radicalism, both in its
intra-state and inter-state manifestations, is nevertheless a
phenomenon that constitutes an acute problem for the United
States, not least because it does not appear amenable to modifica-
tion, let alone eradication. When one state or organization is pre-
vailed upon to temper its radical policies, another state or group
seemingly almost by intuition emerges to take on the challenge and
pursue the struggle. And there seems to be an almost endless supply of radical groups willing, even eager, to fight the good fight.
The conclusion that might be drawn, therefore, is that thus far
radicalism has been an endemic Arab phenomenon. One can even
argue that radicalism-induced conflict seems to be embodied in the
very idea and structure of Arab politics; and that radical states and
organizations, having been at best a nuisance and at worst a
menace for such a long time, have shown the kind of resilience that
does not augur well for the future tranquility and stability of the
area.

Although, as explained in Chapter 5, the persistence of socio-
economic inequities, governmental corruption, and bureaucratic
inefficiencies and mismanagement explain in part the persistence
of Arab radical attitudes and activities, there can be little doubt that
a major contributing factor to Arab radicalism has been the impact
of external forces on Arab politics and society. For example, it was

the effect of the resounding victory of revolutionary Islam in Iran in 1978–79 that gave radical Islam its most potent inspirational drive. Many Arabs saw the overthrow of the Shah and the subsequent humiliation of America as the greatest contemporary victory over the West since the sixteenth and seventeenth centuries when the Ottoman Empire was at its zenith. In the euphoria of 1979, Iran's revolution represented the advent of a new heroic age of assertion and power for Muslims, for Arabs, for the Third World, indeed for all those who resided on the wrong side of the international balance of power. As a result, radical Islamic groups gained new adherents and became more assertive.

In stimulating and fomenting the radical aspirations and activities of the Islamic groups in the Arab world, Iran's revolution is a classic example of the radicalizing effect of an external actor on the politics of Arab countries. But what about the impact on Arab politics of the other major external power in the area, namely Israel? The argument propounded by Israelis and their friends in the United States and in other Western states is that it is through the application of overwhelming force, through the clear exhibition of Israel's strength and resolve, that Arab radicalism against Israel, whether perpetrated by states or groups, is most effectively combatted. They further argue that anti-Israeli radicalism (terrorism is the word they use) diminishes only when radicals, whether states or groups, are made fully aware of the long and heavy hand of Israeli coercive power. To what extent is this argument historically correct?

The historical record is not conclusive. There have been occasions when Israel's military might succeeded in achieving the desired outcome. One of these major successes was Israel's comprehensive defeat of Egypt's Abd al-Nasser and the Syrian neo-Marxist regime in the June 1967 war. The Arab defeat not only spelled the beginning of the end of militant Arab nationalism, but on the state level it also created an ideological milieu that allowed the emergence into political prominence within the Arab world of a group of conservative, status-quo oriented leaders, one of whom was eventually to sign a treaty with the Jewish state. Similarly, Israel's defeat, and consequent expulsion from Lebanon, of the Palestine Liberation Organization in 1982 ended, for all intents and purposes, the PLO's military threat to Israel. In a single devastating blow, the Israelis decimated the PLO's organizational and military infrastructure, dispersed the Palestinian fighters throughout the Arab world, and left Yasser Arafat, 1500 miles away in Tunis, orchestrating a mythical military confrontation with Israel.

On the other hand, the efforts to impose Israel's will by force have also produced countervailing results. For example, while it did undermine revolutionary militancy among Arab states, Israel's stunning June 1967 victory was also directly responsible for the PLO's rise to prominence. The post-1967 weakness of the radical anti-Israeli Arab states, coupled with the Palestinians' awareness that their cause had been left too long in the care of their inadequate Arab brothers, allowed virulent anti-Israeli Palestinian radicalism to move from the periphery to the center of Arab politics for the following decade and a half. Another case in point is Israel's active participation with Britain and France in the 1956 Suez invasion. The operation yielded no territorial gains, yet it catapulted Abd al-Nasser and his radical brand of Arab nationalism into the forefront of Arab politics for the following decade. Until the Iranian revolution in 1979, Suez constituted the single most dramatic radicalizing event in contemporary Arab history.

More recently, the seemingly almost total dependence on force by the Jewish state in its treatment of a quiescent, even in certain instances supportive, Shiite population in the south of Lebanon was the primary contributor to heightened Shiite radicalism, which finally forced Israel to withdraw unilaterally from Lebanon. What could have been a major Israeli victory encapsulating the expulsion of the Palestinians and the securing of Israel's northern border through a cooperative Shiite population ended up as a demoralizing defeat with far-reaching social and moral effects on Israeli society as a whole. Moreover, like the resistance put up by the Palestinian guerrillas in Karameh in 1968, Israel's defeat in South Lebanon resurrected the notion within the Arab world that with the right tactics (guerrilla warfare in 1968, suicidal missions in 1983–85) and the correct faith (Palestinian nationalism in 1968, martyrdom for Islam in 1983–85), Israel's alleged invincibility may be exposed as a myth.

The impact of external actors on Arab radicalism, whatever form it has tended to take, has been considerable. Militant Arab nationalism and its high priest Gamal Abd al-Nasser could not have dominated the political consciousness of the Arabs without the failed tripartite attack on Suez. The echoes of the resurgent march of radical Islam in the late 1970s and early 1980s would not have reached as far and as deep into the Arab psyche had it not been for the triumphant clarion call of the Iranian revolution. In the final analysis, Arab nationalism, Palestinian radicalism and Islamic militancy probably would not have acquired the potency they had, had it not been for the existence of Israel and what Arabs and Muslims have perceived to be its irredentist territorial claims and alien Western culture.

In examining the historical record, therefore, we can reach an understanding of the various domestic and external factors that contribute to the rise or decline of radicalism in the Arab world. Further, history may help us locate some of these factors in order to determine future radical potential. Beyond that, however, history can tell us little about the possible contours of the future development of radical activity. Thus, it cannot tell us when radical sentiment will be harnessed into full revolutionary action. History cannot predict the emergence of a charismatic person, or the eruption of an Iranian-type revolution, or the execution of a seminal military operation such as the 1956 Suez expedition, the 1967 June war or the 1982 Israeli invasion of Lebanon. Yet, the historical record suggests that one or a combination of these occurrences, which are almost impossible to predict through the study of history, need to interact with existing social and economic conditions to produce radical and revolutionary action.

One lesson we can safely draw from the historical record is that success, or at least the perception and aura of success, is essential to the credibility and consequently the persistence and growth of a radical regime or movement. I have cited the role of Nasser's effective stand against the Baghdad Pact and his successful encounter with Britain, France and Israel in 1956 in establishing and then securing his charismatic hold over the Arab radical movement. I have also explained how President Assad's perceived successes in confronting Israel in the wake of its 1982 invasion of Lebanon arrested the steady decline in his mass support suffered as a result of the destruction of Hama earlier that year. But of course the starkest of such examples is the dramatic success of the Iranian revolution, and the impact it had on the growth of Islamic radical movements in the Arab world.

One conceptual difficulty here is that the notion of success is somewhat elastic, which in turn makes it vulnerable to manipulation, even distortion. Thus, for example, the Egyptian armed forces suffered major defeats at the hands of the Israelis in 1956 and 1973. Yet the skilled propagandists of Presidents Nasser and Sadat respectively, ignoring these embarrassing military setbacks, emphasized instead subsequent political gains, elevating them into momentous heroic feats. Similarly, the military encounter between the Palestinians and the Israelis at Karameh in 1968, which perhaps more than any other event led to the phenomenal growth and prestige of the Palestinian guerrillas, in truth was objectively a military defeat for the Palestinians. And it might seem strange to those not familiar with the intricacies of Arab politics that a summary defeat on the ground and the loss of over 80 aircraft in June 1982 could be turned by President Assad into a heroic Syrian victory over Israel and its ally, the United States.

Nebulous and manipulable as the notion of success undoubtedly is, there are instances when even the cleverest of propagandists cannot turn defeat into victory. The consequences of the 1967 Arab-Israeli War were so overwhelmingly disastrous that after a few days of trying to find convenient external scapegoats, the Egyptian government could not but admit that Egypt and the Arab world had suffered a monumental military and political calamity. Similarly, no amount of fiery rhetoric and promises of vengeance could detract from the simple truth that the viability of Palestinian military power had been reduced to near impotence first by Israel and then by Syria in 1982 and 1983.

With the same arguments about success, we can seek to evaluate the future role and power of Islamic radical groups. By its nature, however, this is a controversial method of assessing the power of Islamic militancy, for many will argue that Islam needs no such success to perpetuate itself: successful or not, it will always reside in people's hearts, in their consciousness, in their innermost being, and will always motivate and direct people's attitudes and actions. Muslims will argue that unlike other alien beliefs, such as nationalism, Islam is, and will continue to be, the only authentic ideology around which mass radical opposition can coalesce, regardless of whether it ever succeeds in achieving its declared goals.

It may, however, be sobering to think back to the 1950s and

1960s when the Arab political order was reeling under the assault of revolutionary nationalism. Then, it was not the so-called Islamic revival but Arab socialism that shook the foundation of the moderate Arab political systems; it was not the prospect of the Islamic community but the vision of the pan-Arab republic that dominated the psyche of the masses; it was not the clerical Khomeini of Islamic Iran but the secular Nasser of nationalist Egypt who embodied the essence of the revolutionary march.

My argument is that Islamic militancy today is no more permanent and no less transient than the Arab nationalism of yesterday. Thus I start from an altogether different premise. I hold to the view that the faith or dogma of a mass movement is not the central issue; what really matters is the hope that the movement is able to provide. And hope is intrinsically, almost causally, linked to success. This is why the Arab nationalist movement flourished after hopes were raised sky high by the 1956 Suez success, and then declined when hopes were dashed after the June 1967 disaster. Again, this is why the Islamic revival reached its euphoric peak in the early 1980s in the wake of the "miracle" of the Iranian revolution which had inflated Arab/Muslim hopes for an Islamic take-over of political power and the consequent institution of a just social order.

The success of Iran's Islamic revolution was without doubt the major catalyst for greater radical activism among militant Arab Islamic groups. In November 1979, armed followers of a Sunni Muslim extremist group occupied the Grand Mosque in Mecca. The siege continued for over two weeks of bloody battle with Saudi security forces until the militants were finally defeated. Simultaneously, there were a number of riots by members of the Shiite community in Saudi Arabia's Eastern province. Islamic fundamentalism spread through Arab schools and universities, becoming the springboard for active and vociferous agitation against the established political orders in such countries as Jordan, Morocco, Bahrain, Sudan and Tunisia. In Iraq, the mounting acts of subversion by the pro-Iranian Da'wa party constituted an important catalyst in President Saddam Hussein's decision to go to war against Iran in September 1980. The assassination of President Sadat by the extremist Tanzim al-Gihad group in October 1981 was further proof of the rising power of Islamic militancy—a radical onslaught that threatened to swamp pro-Soviet as well as pro-American Arab leadership, as the "leftist" President Assad of Syria was to discover in early 1982 when a determined group of Muslim Brothers staged a bloody mini-rebellion in the Syrian city of Hama.

It is my belief, however, that the tide of militant Islamic fundamentalism reached its peak during the three-year period, February 1979-February 1982. Since then, Islamic revolutionary fervor seems to have waned as success continued to elude those who had been proclaiming inevitable victory for Islamic militancy and the promised salvation of the Arab Muslim people. In no Arab country have the Muslim radicals been able to emulate the success of the Iranian uprising against the Shah. Indeed, in all the cases cited above involving a confrontation between the state and Islamic revolution, the Muslim militants were soundly defeated by overwhelming state power.

Perhaps even more damaging to the prestige of militant Islam has been the Iranian mullahs' war with Iraq. True, Iran has survived the conflict. Through a fusion of patriotism, religious orthodoxy, and military pragmatism, Iran turned what appeared to be a runaway Iraqi victory at the outset into a ruinous war of attrition that has gradually turned Iran's way. But the non-Iranian Muslim remembers well how, at the outset of the war, the Iranian clergy had confidently predicted that the Iraqi Muslim soldiers would soon revolt against the "worthless infidel who opposes Islam." The message to Saddam Hussein from Tehran was clear and confident:

> God will defeat your devices. In the coming days you will learn how the Muslim people and army of beloved Iraq will respond to you, and how the Muslim Iranian army and people will respond to you. You will know how you have dug your own grave—the grave of shame and humiliation in this world, and the grave of hellfire in the hereafter.[4]

The ensuing bloody stalemate in the war was inevitably damaging to Khomeini's prestige. It must be remembered that in the minds of Muslims, a crucial difference existed between the secularist Hussein of Iraq and the spiritual, to some even "divine," ayatollah. While Hussein fought the war with mechanical devices such as airplanes and tanks, Khomeini's devices were mystical, employing the power of God and his angels. Hussein, therefore, unleashed a power against Iran whose failures and frailties were recognized and understood; Khomeini's power, on the other hand, by its very mystical definition, should not have any frailties.

Nor were the ayatollahs capable of achieving the one thing that they and their followers and admirers had so confidently hoped for, even predicted—Hussein's overthrow by the Shiites of Iraq. The Arab Muslims, even the Shiites, must have wondered frequently throughout this senseless war why it was taking the "divine" ayatollah such a long time to dispose of the "worthless infidel." Surely Iraq should have been the ayatollahs' most fertile ground: the only other Muslim country where the ethnically Arab Shiites actually formed a majority, the next-door neighbor to Iran in which Khomeini himself had spent 14 years in exile from the Shah.

Whatever the ultimate outcome of the war, the failure of Iran and its clerical leaders to win a decisive victory and incite the Iraqi Shiites to rebellion means that, while future battles may be won or lost by the Iranian military, the Iranian revolution lost its war long ago and was diminished as a result.

Khomeiniism, as a symbol of Islamic rejuvenation, as a standard by which Arab Muslims evaluate their own political leaderships, is no longer the threat to Arab stability it was in the heyday of the Iranian revolution. The loss of potency is evident in Iran's own behavior. Whereas in the past the clergy's influence emanated from the virility of their mystical and religious symbolism, they now increasingly resort to war and to physical acts of subversion in order to assert their power. During their days of glory, it was the impact of the spoken and written word that shook the very foundations of the neighboring countries. Now the ayatollahs are reduced to behaving like mortals: they send troops and train guerrillas and still cannot induce the required changes in the neighboring countries.

But perhaps most disappointing has been the abysmal performance of the Islamic republic in Iran. There is little doubt that the revolution has stalled: its atrocities have penetrated the mist of Tehran's propaganda to depict a reality which does not correspond to the ayatollahs' sterling claims. As a result, the early euphoria of the Muslim masses is quickly turning into disillusion—not so much in Iran itself, since as makers of the revolution, Iranians are likely to cling to the last vestiges of hope that the revolution will be redeemed, that it will soon deliver, that it will triumph in the end. Meanwhile, they are still prepared to fight, even die, for the ideals of the revolution. But those on the other side of the Gulf have not physically lived through the revolutionary experience; they have neither endured the pain, nor experienced the ecstasy, and so they are more fickle, more impatient, and less committed. Arab Muslims now are hedging their bets, waiting to see whether someone, a Mahdi perhaps, can rescue the faltering revolution.

In this lie the signs of the gradual decline as well as the ultimate failure of Islamic militancy; for once the power of the moral inspiration begins to be questioned, it is only a matter of time before the flock begins to reach for other alternatives. It was thus part of this general trend that in Kuwait's parliamentary elections held in February 1985, Muslim fundamentalists lost considerable ground, whereas nationalists, who had been heavily defeated in 1981, were returned with increasing strength. Perhaps the writing was on the wall when, a year earlier, the editor of a leading Islamic magazine in Kuwait confided that his country's neighbors (no doubt with Iran in mind) did not "need more Islam but more political liberties."[5] Dramatic acts like assassinations and suicide missions, perpetrated by Muslim activists, will no doubt continue to occur. However, the prospects for fundamental restructuring of social and political systems according to Islamic prescriptions are much dimmer today than they were four or five years earlier when Iran's revolution was still considered a success, and its politicians could still masquerade as inspired and humane leaders.

It therefore seems that the one conclusion that can be extrapolated from a study of the history of radicalism in the Arab world, and used to predict the future fortune of a contemporary radical state or movement, is that success, or more precisely the perception of success, is an important, even critical, factor in making or breaking the state or the organization in question. In the case of the radical Arab states, legitimacy cannot be attained and maintained without a healthy dose of successful policies and ventures. Radical movements are likewise dependent on success to nourish constantly the hopes and aspirations of their followers, so essential to keeping the loyalty and unity of the flock. True, a radical act is a manifestation of the ideology and political orientation of the radical state or organization; but it is also an effort to maintain the legitimacy of the radical leaders and the raison d'être of the state or movement in question. At the intra-state level, the radical act be-

comes also the vehicle through which peoples' demands for redressing chronic socio-economic and political inequities can take
shape and be felt by the political and economic elites.

Radical activity, therefore, has not been just a policy instrument that could easily be discarded, nor has it been a transient political orientation dictated solely by tactical considerations. Rather,
Arab radicalism has been a mode of political self-expression as well
as a necessary condition for political survival, which is embodied in
the very structure, no less than the discourse, of Arab politics. Does
this then mean that intra-state and inter-state Arab radicalism will
not decrease or be contained in the future?

A glance at the Iraq-Iran war may help to answer this question.
Western paranoia about terrorism today is nothing compared with
what it might have been if Iraq had fallen to the committed soldiers
of Islam, and if Iran had been able to swarm the sparsely populated
expanse of Saudi Arabia and the Gulf with thousands of its fist-
clenching Shiite zealots. But the Iraqi political order survived; and it
survived not only because of its tight control of Iraqi society, or because of the Iranians' own shortcomings, but also because of the
prudent policies of Iraq's leaders. The mid- and late 1970s saw President Hussein and the Baath Party use much of the massive oil re-
turns to bridge the gap between rich and poor in Iraq. Numerous
economic and social policies, such as social security systems, pension plans, minimum wages, free health and education, were
enacted in order to bring the excluded into the mainstream of Iraqi
society.

Socially equitable this policy certainly was. But more important
for Iraq's leadership, it was politically astute, for the majority of
Iraq's poor have traditionally belonged to the Shiite faith. And it is
to those very Shiites of Iraq that Khomeini's calls for rebellion have
been specifically directed throughout the Iraq-Iran war. Iran's failure to incite even a minor Shiite insurrection in Iraq owes as much
to the social and economic policies of Hussein and the Iraqi leadership as to the plummeting prestige of the aging Ayatollah. Other
Arab leaders, concerned about the potential for radical upheavals in
their countries, can take a leaf from Iraq's book and endeavour to reduce socio-economic disparities as one incisive method of curtailing
the radical threat to their political orders.

Beyond trying to bridge socio-economic disparities, Arab leaders, concerned about radicalism, could do worse than to allow their people more real and effective participation in the political process. Rather than maintaining their countries as bastions of American and Western influence in the area, the moderate Arab kings and presidents could better withstand the onslaught of their radical Arab "brothers" if they allowed their own people to have a greater stake in the political system.

The message seems to be getting through. A number of moderate Arab regimes during the first half of the 1980s undertook democratic experiments to liberalize the ultra-centralization of their political orders. Morocco, Tunisia, Kuwait, Jordan and Egypt all conducted relatively free elections, and the new legislative assemblies provided in most cases vigorous political debates and in some instances determined opposition to governmental policies and strictures.

Of course, like a baby's first steps, these democratic experiments have been tentative and imperfect, impeded by uncertainty about the next step. Without doubt, a number of incidents during the election campaigns and later during parliamentary debates betrayed the rulers' intense distaste for relinquishing absolute power and their seemingly chronic mistrust of their people. But, at the same time, these early efforts at political liberalization seem to be a way for political leaders to test the waters; to balance in their own minds the benefits that would accrue to them in terms of increased popularity and a lessening of peoples' political frustrations against the possible costs of public and vociferous opposition. After all, given their pervasive power, there was no need for these leaders to allow even this limited liberalization of their political systems had they not suspected that people were no longer satisfied with the current order of things, with being talked at rather than talked with, with being constantly patronized.

But primarily the process of gradual democratization acts as a safety valve against the growth of radicalism. In a recent interview, President Mubarak confidently declared that the radical Islamic tide was beginning to ebb in Egypt. He said that he would continue to permit the Islamicists and others who criticize the government to speak out, and maintained that his policy had helped stem the growth of the radical forces in Egypt. "It is called democracy," President Mubarak asserted; "if you suppress these forces, they will spread much more."[6]

Other Arab leaders, radicals and non-radicals alike, will do well to reflect on Mubarak's words. The choice for these leaders is a stark one: they can give way and gradually allow people more freedom and greater democracy, taking a chance in the process that the people, of their own free will, will return them to power. Alternatively, they can put the brakes on, ensuring the elimination of public opposition but running the risk that people will vent their political frustrations increasingly through radical, subversive and revolutionary channels.

Only the hopelessly optimistic would forecast that democracy is destined to triumph over radicalism. For even if leaders and regimes genuinely decide to go down the road of democratic liberalization, there will remain many internal and external factors which will continue to nourish radical impulses. The enduring (in some cases increasing) socio-economic disparities and inequities, the chronic bureaucratic inefficiencies and mismanagement, the persistence of corruption in high places, the Arab-Israeli conflict and other regional conflicts, the efforts by outside powers to extend their influence in the region, the persistent destabilizing potency of such transnational forces as Arabism and Islam, and the competition among Arab states and their leaders for security, power and prestige will continue to fan the flames of radicalism. On the other hand, there is heightened awareness by Arab leaders that liberalizing their political orders and allowing more active political participation makes their people less susceptible to radical and revolutionary calls domestically or from the outside.

Perhaps they that take up the sword either triumph or perish by the sword; but if the cutting edge of revolutionary radicalism is blunted by democratic reforms, then perhaps even the radical gladiators may eventually be persuaded to give up the sword.

Appendix

Appendix   Significant Radical Acts in the Arab World, 1970–1986

	THE RADICAL STATES	THE RADICAL MOVEMENTS: THE PLO	THE RELIGIOUS RADICAL MOVEMENTS
1970–1976	South Yemen actively supports the Marxist guerrilla forces in the Dhofar province of the Sultanate of Muscat and Oman.		
September 1970		Palestinian commandos hijack three civil airliners to a desert air strip in Jordan—an action that leads to the Jordanian civil war, which results in hundreds of Palestinian casualties and the expulsion of the PLO from Jordan.	
1971–June 1982		The PLO wages its war against Israel from the south of Lebanon through guerrilla infiltration, bombardment and rocket attacks.	
1971		The Palestinian guerrillas are involved in numerous acts of terror (assassinations, hijacking of planes and ships, hostage-taking, bomb attacks, etc.) principally against Israeli and American, but also in some cases Arab, targets. The most consequential of these acts were perhaps the following:	

	THE RADICAL STATES	*THE RADICAL MOVEMENTS: THE PLO*	*THE RELIGIOUS RADICAL MOVEMENTS*
November 1971		Jordanian Premier Wasfi al-Tel, held responsible by the PLO for the civil war, is assassinated by members of the Black September organization.	
May 1972		Three Japanese men associated with the PFLP open fire at Lod airport in Tel Aviv killing 26 and wounding 70.	
September 1972		The Black September organization holds the Israeli Olympic team hostage in Munich. In a later battle with German authorities, 11 Israelis and 5 guerrillas are killed.	
September–October 1972	War between South Yemen and North Yemen flares up after intermittent fighting between the two countries that had begun in early 1971.		
December 1972	Iraqi military troops cross the border into Kuwait to protect a construction crew, which begins to build a road leading to the Gulf in Kuwaiti territory.		
March 1973	Iraqi troops occupy a Kuwaiti police station at Samitha, with a number of Kuwaiti casualties.		

	THE RADICAL STATES	THE RADICAL MOVEMENTS: THE PLO	THE RELIGIOUS RADICAL MOVEMENTS
March 1973–June 1982		The PLO is intermittently (and after 1975 almost constantly) engaged in military confrontation with the Christian-dominated Lebanese army and the Christian Maronite militia, the Phalanges.	
October 1973	Egypt and Syria launch the October 1973 War against Israel.		
April 1974			Al-Tahrir al-Islami (Islamic Liberation) attacks the military technical academy in Cairo, Egypt, and in a pitched battle with Egyptian security-forces, 11 persons are killed and 27 wounded.
November–December 1974	Iraqi troops infiltrate Kuwaiti territory and set up military posts.		
December 1975		An obscure Libyan-supported Palestinian group storms the OPEC headquarters in Vienna and holds 60 people, including 11 OPEC delegates, hostage. The hostages are then released in Algiers and Tripoli.	
1976–	Algeria begins and maintains its diplomatic and material support for the claims of Polisario against Morocco in the Western Sahara, which has led to some direct clashes between Algeria and Morocco.		

	THE RADICAL STATES	THE RADICAL MOVEMENTS: THE PLO	THE RELIGIOUS RADICAL MOVEMENTS
June 1976–	The Syrian armed forces enter Lebanon in order to terminate the Lebanese civil war. Syrian armed forces have remained in Lebanon since then.		
June–July 1976		Members of the PFLP organization hijack a plane and direct it to Entebbe airport in Uganda. They demand the release of 53 imprisoned Palestinians in Israeli jails. An Israeli commando unit raids Entebbe airport and frees the hostages. Four Israelis, 7 guerrillas and 20 soldiers are killed.	
July 1977	Fighting breaks out between Libyan and Egyptian troops, including aerial bombings.		
October 1977		PFLP guerrillas hijack a West German airliner and direct it to Mogadishu in Somalia, demanding the release of Palestinians from German and Turkish jails. West German commandos storm the plane and release the passengers. All guerrillas are killed.	

	THE RADICAL STATES	THE RADICAL MOVEMENTS: THE PLO	THE RELIGIOUS RADICAL MOVEMENTS
1977–March 1978			Al-Takfir Wal-Higra (Repentence and Holy Flight) kidnaps and later kills a former Egyptian minister of religious endowments. Following the incident, a number of clashes between al-Takfir and Egyptian security forces occur that lead to the arrest of 400 sympathizers and the execution of 5 leaders.
March 1978		Al-Fateh guerrillas land on a beach in Israel, seize a bus, and fight a battle with security forces. The attack leaves 34 Israelis, 1 American and 9 Palestinian dead.	
June 1978	A bomb explodes in the bag of a South Yemeni envoy, killing the President of North Yemen, Ahmad Ghashemi.		
February–March 1979	South Yemeni forces enter North Yemen and capture a number of border villages. Fighting continues until an agreement is reached in Kuwait on March 29.		
June 1979			Muslim Brothers raid a military academy in the northern Syrian city of Aleppo, killing 32 and wounding 54 cadets, all of whom are members of the Alawite sect.

	THE RADICAL STATES	*THE RADICAL MOVEMENTS: THE PLO*	*THE RELIGIOUS RADICAL MOVEMENTS*
January 1980	Libyan-trained Tunisian dissidents take over the Tunisian town of Gafsa, surrendering it only after heavy fighting with Tunisian security forces that results in 41 dead and 11 injured.		
March–April 1980			Two bomb attacks by members of al-Da'wa (The Call) party on Iraqi leaders and personnel lead to the execution of Imam Baqir al-Sadr, the most influential Shiite cleric in Iraq, and to the expulsion of 35,000 Iraqi Shiites to Iran.
November–December 1980	Syria deploys 20,000 troops and 400 tanks on its border with Jordan, and threatens to invade unless Jordan stops supporting the Syrian Muslim Brothers.		
October 1981			Tanzim al-Gihad (The Holy War Organization) assassinates President Anwar al-Sadat of Egypt, and precipitates a mini-insurrection in the southern Egyptian city of Assyut.
December 1981			A massive explosion, perpetrated by al-Da'wa, destroys the Iraqi embassy in West Beirut, killing 27 and wounding over 100.

	THE RADICAL STATES	THE RADICAL MOVEMENTS: THE PLO	THE RELIGIOUS RADICAL MOVEMENTS
February 1982			Over 500 heavily armed members of the Syrian Islamic Front take over the Syrian city of Hama. During three weeks of savage battles with Syrian security forces, thousands of people are killed and almost half of the city is razed to the ground.
June 1982		Israel's ambassador to Great Britain is critically wounded by a fringe Palestinian group. Israel uses the attack as a pretext for its invasion of Lebanon.	
June 1982	Syria engages the invading Israeli forces in battles on the ground and in the air in Lebanon.		
April 1983			The Lebanese Shiite Islamic Jihad plants a bomb that destroys the U.S. embassy in Beirut, killing 63 people and wounding close to 100.
May 1983	Syria opposes the American-sponsored Lebanese-Israeli agreement, which eventually leads to the unilateral abrogation of the treaty by Lebanon in March 1984.		

September–
December 1983

Syrian forces attack pro-Arafat
Palestinian fighters in Tripoli in northern
Lebanon, leading to the evacuation of
4,000 Palestinians, including Yasser
Arafat, from Tripoli on Greek ships
under French protection.

October 1983

A truck loaded with explosives, driven
by members of Islamic Jihad, crashes
through the headquarters of the U.S.
Marine battalion in Beirut; 241 marines
lose their lives. A similar attack on the
French quarters kills 58 soldiers.

November 1983

A suicidal car bomb attack, engineered
by Islamic Jihad, on Israeli headquarters
in Tyre, Lebanon, kills 61 people, of
whom 28 are Israeli soldiers.

December 1983

Shiite Muslims of Lebanese and Iraqi
extraction are involved in blowing up
the American embassy compound in
Kuwait, killing 5 people and
wounding 62.

September 1983–
February 1984

Syrian and American forces
intermittently exchange fire, including
the shooting down over Lebanese
territory by Syrian artillery of two
American planes. In February 1984,
American troops, exposed to Syrian
forces and their allies, the Druze and
Shiite militia, withdraw from Lebanon.

February 1984

The Shiite Amal militia, aided by its
Druze allies, defeats units of the
Lebanese army and takes control of
West Beirut. This action precipitates
the disintegration of the American-
trained and equipped Lebanese army.

May 1985

The Amal militiamen attack PLO
concentrations in Beirut and Tyre in an
effort to prevent a resurgence of
Palestinian power in Lebanon.

June 1985

Constant Shiite pressure compels
Israel to withdraw unilaterally from
Lebanon.

June 1985

Shiite gunmen hijack a TWA jetliner
bound from Athens to Rome, forcing it
to land in Beirut and Algiers before
returning to Beirut. One passenger is
killed and 39 hostages are kept in
captivity for 17 days. Hijackers demand
the release of about 800 Lebanese

THE RADICAL STATES	THE RADICAL MOVEMENTS: THE PLO	THE RELIGIOUS RADICAL MOVEMENTS
1985–1986		Heavy intermittent fighting between Amal and Palestinian militias in Beirut leaves hundreds dead. The Shiite Hizbollah group join the fighting on the side of the Palestinians against the Shiite Amal.
October 1985	Israeli jets attack PLO headquarters in Tunis, killing 30–50 people and wounding more, including Tunisian civilians, in retaliation against the murder in Larnaca, Cyprus of three Israelis by the PLO elite Force 17.	
October 1985	Palestinian commandos hijack an Italian cruise ship, the Achille Lauro, off the coast of Egypt. The hijackers demand the release of Palestinian prisoners in Israel. An American passenger is killed. The hijackers then surrender unconditionally to Egyptian officials and a PLO representative. The Egyptian plane returning the hijackers to PLO headquarters in Tunisia is intercepted by U.S. Navy warplanes and forced to land in Italy.	

THE RADICAL MOVEMENTS:
THE PLO

THE RADICAL STATES

December 1985

In apparently coordinated grenade and
machine-gun attacks on El-Al Israel
Airlines check-in counters at Rome
and Vienna airports, terrorists kill at
least 12 and wound many more. The
Palestinian dissident group headed by
Abu Nidhal is implicated. The attack
is allegedly a reprisal for the Israeli
raid on Tunis in October.

March 1986

Libyan ground forces fire six missiles
at American planes inside the Gulf of
Sidra. U.S. warplanes retaliate by
attacking a number of Libyan patrol
boats and SAM-5 missile sites on
Libyan soil at Sirte. About 60 are
reportedly killed.

April 1986

A bomb in a West Berlin discotheque
kills two American soldiers and injures
80 others, mostly Americans. The U.S.
blames Libya, and carries out a bombing
raid on Libyan airfields, command
posts, and suspected terrorist camps
around Tripoli and Benghazi. Many
civilians are reported killed and
wounded in the raids, which hit at
least one residential neighborhood
in Tripoli.

Notes

CHAPTER 1

1. John Locke, *Two Treatises of Government* (London: Cambridge University Press, 1960).
2. See *The Middle East and North Africa*, 31st edition (London: Europa Publications Ltd., 1984), pp. 201–202.
3. For a longer exposition of this theme, see Adeed Dawisha, "Anti-Americanism in the Arab World: Memories of the Past in the Attitudes of the Future," in Alvin Z. Rubinstein and Donald E. Smith, eds. *Anti-Americanism in the Third World: Implications for U.S. Foreign Policy* (New York: Praeger, 1985), pp. 67–84.
4. See Adeed Dawisha, "The Soviet Union and the Arab World: The Limits to Superpower Influence," in Adeed Dawisha and Karen Dawisha, eds., *The Soviet Union in the Middle East: Policies and Perspectives* (New York: Holmes and Meier, 1982), pp. 8–23.
5. These groups take their cue from the Iranian revolution in which Soviet "satanic evil" is second only to that of the United States.
6. Maxime Rodinson, *The Arabs* (London: Croom Helm, 1981), p. 25.
7. Sad al-Din Ibrahim, *Itijahat al-Ra'y al-Am al-Arabi Nahwa Mas'alat al-Wuhda* [Arab Public Opinion Attitudes towards the Issue of Unity] (Beirut: Merkaz Dirasat al-Wuhda al-Arabiya, 1980).
8. For a dissenting view which drew on another, albeit a more limited, opinion survey, see Fouad Ajami, "The End of Pan-Arabism," *Foreign Affairs,* Winter 1978–79, pp. 355–72.

CHAPTER 2

1. Geoffrey Barraclough, *An Introduction to Contemporary History* (Harmondsworth: Penguin Books, 1967), p. 16.
2. Anthony Nutting, *The Arabs* (New York: Mentor Books, 1964), p. 126.
3. Quoted in Bernard Lewis, *The Arabs in History* (New York: Harper and Row Publishers, 1966), p. 165.
4. Quoted in Norman Daniel, *Islam, Europe and Empire* (Edinburgh: Edinburgh University Press, 1966), p. 552.
5. Albert Hourani, *Arabic Thought in the Liberal Age 1798–1939* (London: Oxford University Press, 1970), p. 120.
6. See Edward Said, *Orientalism* (New York: Vintage Books, 1978).

7. See, for example, Dwight D. Eisenhower, *The White House Years: Vol. II, Waging Peace* (New York: Doubleday, 1965), p. 197.

8. *Al-Ahram* (Cairo), February 24, 1967.

9. The aura of Nasser's charisma, it seems, reached beyond the Arab domain into as unlikely a place as the Shiite holy city of Qom in Iran. See Roy Mottahedeh's brilliant *The Mantle of the Prophet: Religion and Politics in Iran* (New York: Simon and Schuster, 1985), pp. 114–115.

10. *Al-Ahram* (Cairo), December 29, 1961.

CHAPTER 3

1. Anthoine Guinea, *The New Syria* (Damascus: S.A.M.A., 1975), p. 103.

2. Quoted in Majid Khadduri, *Socialist Iraq: A Study in Iraqi Politics Since 1968* (Washington, D.C.: The Middle East Institute, 1978), p. 208.

3. See Adeed Dawisha, *Egypt in the Arab World: The Elements of Foreign Policy* (New York: The Halsted Press, 1976), p. 89.

4. Charles Issawi, *An Arab Philosopher of History* (London: John Murray, 1950), p. 114.

5. Hamilton Gibb, "Constitutional Organization: The Muslim Community and the State," in Majid Khadduri and Herbert Liebesny, eds., *Law in the Middle East* (Washington, D.C.: Middle East Institute, 1955), p. 15.

6. Albert Hourani, *Arabic Thought in the Liberal Age, 1798–1939* (London: Oxford University Press, 1962), p. 14.

7. Majid Khadduri, *War and Peace in the Law of Islam* (Baltimore: The Johns Hopkins University Press, 1955), p. 12.

8. See Adeed Dawisha, *Syria and the Lebanese Crisis* (New York: St. Martin's Press, 1980), pp. 102–103.

9. *Al-Thawra* (Baghdad), June 29, 1982.

10. *Africa Now*, February 1983, pp. 42–43.

11. *Africa Contemporary Record, 1979–1980*, pp. 23–27, quoted in Bahgat Korany, "Third Worldism and Pragmatic Radicalism: The Foreign Policy of Algeria," in Bahgat Korany and Ali E. Hillal Dessouki, *The Foreign Policies of Arab States* (Boulder, Colorado: Westview Press, 1984), p. 86.

12. This section draws on information provided by Norman Cigar in his paper for the Council's study group.

13. *Al-Siyassa* (Kuwait), June 28, 1984.

14. *Africa Now*, February 1963, p. 45.

15. Mirella Bianco, *Gadafi: Voice From the Desert* (London: Longman, 1975), p. 19.

16. *Al-Thawra* (Baghdad), July 17, 1980.

17. Quoted in Adeed Dawisha, *Egypt in the Arab World*, p. 131.

18. *Al-Thawra* (Baghdad), September 18, 1980.

19. *Al-Thawra* (Baghdad), March 23, 1974.

20. British Broadcasting Corporation, *Summary of World Broadcasts, Part IV, The Middle East*, ME/5021/A/1, October 1, 1975.

CHAPTER 4

1. *Al-Mu'tamar al-Istithnai' lil Hizb al-Ishtiraki al-Yemeni* (The Extraordinary Congress of the Yemeni Socialist Party), (Beirut: Dar Ibn Khaldun, 1980), p. 113 (hereafter cited as Mu'tamar)

2. *The Middle East*, May 1978, p. 24.

3. Richard A. Roughton, "Algeria and the June 1967 Arab-Israeli War," *Middle East Journal*, Autumn 1969, p. 444.

4. British Broadcasting Corporation, *Summary of World Broadcasts, Part IV, The Middle East and Africa*, ME/5267/A/4, July 22, 1976.

5. Adeed Dawisha, *Syria and the Lebanese Crisis* (New York: St. Martin's Press, 1980).

6. Quoted in Hassan Muhamed Tawalibah, *al-Qadhiya al-Qawmiya bein al-Manhaj al-Kifahi wal Tadhlil al-Maqsood* (The Nationalist Question Between the Program of Revolutionary Struggle and Deliberate Falsification), (Baghdad: Wizarat al-Thaqafa wal I'lam, 1980), pp. 101–105.

7. *Al-Thawra* (Baghdad), September 18, 1980.

8. *Al-Safir* (Beirut), March 21, 1981.

9. Lisa Anderson, "Libya and American Foreign Policy," *Middle East Journal*, Autumn 1982, pp. 531–32.

10. Fouad Ajami, *The Arab Predicament: Arab Political Thought and Practice Since 1967* (Cambridge, England: Cambridge University Press, 1981), p. 85.

11. *Al-Thawra* (Baghdad), April 17, 1980.

12. Indeed, these work remittances totalled $411 million in 1982, which was equivalent to 44 percent of the country's GNP of $940 million. See The World Bank, *World Development Report, 1984* (Oxford: Oxford University Press, 1984), table 14.

13. *Pravda*, April 2, 1984.

14. British Broadcasting Corporation, *Summary of World Broadcasts, Part IV The Middle East and Africa*, ME/7278/A/5, March 10, 1983.

15. Dawisha, *Syria and The Lebanese Crisis*, pp. 169–170.

16. *International Herald Tribune*, October 12, 1982.

17. Quoted in Karen Dawisha, "The U.S.S.R. in the Middle East: Superpower in Eclipse?", *Foreign Affairs*, Winter 1982–83, p. 445.

18. Anderson, *op. cit.*, p. 526.

19. Bahgat Korany and Ali E. Hillal Dessouki, *The Foreign Policies of Arab States* (Boulder, Colorado: Westview Press, 1984), p. 105.

20. *Keesings Contemporary Archives, 1980*, p. 30242.

21. *Mu'tamar*, p. 102.

22. Quoted in I. William Zartman and A.G. Kluge, "Heroic Politics: The Foreign Policy of Libya," in Korany and Dessouki, *op. cit.*, p. 189.

23. Quoted in Adeed Dawisha, "The Stability of the Gulf: Domestic Sources and External Threats," in Alvin Z. Rubinstein, ed., *The Great Game: Rivalry in the Persian Gulf and South Asia* (New York: Praeger, 1983), pp. 18–19.

CHAPTER 5

1. This section draws on information provided by Rashid Khalidi in his paper for the Council's study group.

2. Quoted in Mohamed E. Selim, "The Survival of a Nonstate Actor: The Foreign Policy of the Palestinian Liberation Organization," in Bahgat Korany and Ali E. Hillal Dessouki, *The Foreign Policies of Arab States* (Boulder, Colorado: The Westview Press, 1984), pp. 202–203.

3. *Ibid.,* pp. 207–208.

4. *The New York Times,* November 20, 1984.

5. *Keesing's Contemporary Archives, 1985,* p. 32233.

6. Hamied N. Ansari, "The Islamic Militants in Egyptian Politics," *International Journal of Middle Eastern Studies,* March 1984, p. 126.

7. For a thorough analysis of the various Shiite opposition groups, see Hana Batatu, "Iraq's Underground Shi'a Movements: Characteristics, Causes and Prospects," *Middle East Journal,* Autumn 1981, pp. 578–94.

8. The characterization of Imam Sadr draws on Augustus Richard Norton's paper for the Council's study group on the Arab radicals. See also Fouad Ajami, "Lebanon and Its Inheritors," *Foreign Affairs,* Spring 1985, pp. 779–84.

9. See R. Hrair Dekmejian, *Islam in Revolution: Fundamentalism in the Arab World* (New York: Syracuse University Press, 1985), pp. 120–21.

10. Quoted in *Ibid.,* pp. 116–17.

11. *The Washington Post,* December 5, 1982.

12. *Le Monde* (Paris), March 22, 1984.

13. *Monday Morning,* October 15–21, 1984, pp. 40–45.

14. Quoted in Ajami, *op. cit.,* p. 792.

15. See, for example, Hamied Ansari, "The Islamic Militants in Egyptian Politics," *International Journal of Middle Eastern Studies*, March 1984, pp. 123–44.

16. See Majid Khadduri, *The Islamic Conception of Justice* (Baltimore: The Johns Hopkins University Press, 1984).

CHAPTER 6

1. *Al-Wathaiq al-Siyyassiya al-Arabiya, 1967* (Arab Political Documents), (Beirut, American University of Beirut, n.d.), p. 718.

2. *Al-Ahram* (Cairo), August 16, 1968.

3. This concern had been a primary reason for Syria's initial intervention in June 1976. See President Assad's interview with *Events,* October 1, 1976, p. 20.

4. *Al-Yawm* (Beirut), December 24, 1983.

5. *The New York Times,* December 4, 1983.

6. IISS, *Strategic Survey, 1984–85,* p. 64.

7. *Keesings Contemporary Archives,* Vol. 31, p. 33494.

8. Hamied N. Ansari, "The Islamic Militants in Egyptian Politics," *International Journal of Middle Eastern Studies,* March 1984, p. 126.

9. British Broadcasting Corporation, *Summary of World Broadcasts, Part IV, the Middle East and Africa,* ME/5185/A/6, April 14, 1976.

10. Malise Ruthven, "Islamic Politics in the Middle East," in *The Middle East and North Africa, 1984–85,* p. 127.

11. *Al-Thawra* (Baghdad), April 2, 1982.

12. Quoted in Fouad Ajami, "Lebanon and Its Inheritors," *Foreign Affairs,* Spring 1985, p. 785.

13. *Al-Nahar* (Beirut), November 5, 1983.

CHAPTER 7

1. See the interview with Sayyid Muhammed Hussein Fadlallah in *al-Hawadith* (Beirut), May 23, 1986, p. 14.

2. *The Washington Post,* August 19, 1985.

3. *The Washington Post*, May 18, 1986.

4. British Broadcasting Corporation, *Summary of World Broadcasts, Part 4, The Middle East and Africa,* ME/6531/A/7, September 24, 1980.

5. *The Washington Post,* May 3, 1984.

6. *The New York Times,* February 25, 1985.

Index

About the Author

Adeed Dawisha is Professor of Government and Politics at George Mason University in Fairfax, Virginia. Born in Baghdad, Iraq, Dr. Dawisha received his Ph.D. from the London School of Economics and Political Science in 1974. He subsequently taught at a number of British universities. In 1977–78, he was a Senior Research Associate at the London-based International Institute for Strategic Studies. In 1979, he joined the Royal Institute of International Affairs as Deputy Director of Studies. On leave from the Institute during 1983–85, he was first Visiting Professor at The School of Advanced International Studies, The Johns Hopkins University, and then Visiting Fellow at the Department of Near Eastern Studies, Princeton University, and Consulting Fellow at the Council on Foreign Relations, New York City. During 1985–86, he was Fellow at the Woodrow Wilson International Center for Scholars of the Smithsonian Institution.

In addition to over 50 book chapters and articles in scholarly journals, Dr. Dawisha is the author of *Egypt in the Arab World: The Elements of Foreign Policy* (Macmillan and Wiley, 1976), *Syria and The Lebanese Crisis* (Macmillan and St. Martin's Press, 1980), and *Saudi Arabia's Search for Security* (International Institute for Strategic Studies, 1980—translated into Japanese 1980, into German 1981). He is also the editor (with Karen Dawisha) of *The Soviet Union in the Middle East: Policies and Perspectives* (Heinemann and Holmes and Meier, 1982), and *Islam in Foreign Policy* (Cambridge University Press, 1983).

Dr. Dawisha has also contributed articles to *The New York Times, The Times* (London), and a number of Arabic-language magazines and newspapers. He has also appeared on the evening news programs of ABC, NBC, and CBS Television Networks, as well as on the MacNeil-Lehrer News Hour.

gon radicalism –

Valente

Psultahis – Bt